THE *Lyric* Library

Early Rock 'n' Roll

Complete Lyrics for 200 Songs

HAL•LEONARD®

ISBN 0-634-04483-4

Library of Congress cataloguing-in-publication data has been applied for.

Visit Hal Leonard Online at
www.halleonard.com

Preface

Songs have an uncanny ability to burrow deep into our gray matter, sometimes lying dormant for years or decades before something pings them back into our consciousness. All kinds of songs reside in there, more than we can count—not just songs we love and intentionally memorized and have sung again and again, but songs we once heard in passing, songs that form a soundtrack to significant people and places and moments in our lives, and even (or especially) songs that drive us crazy, like the chirping TV jingle that still won't let go years after the product it plugged has disappeared from the shelves.

Most of the time, though, our memories of songs are frustratingly incomplete unless we actively maintain them. The first verse and chorus that we blare out in the shower or at the jam session degenerates into mumbled lines, disconnected phrases, and bits and pieces inadvertently lifted from other songs. And, of course, there's the likelihood that what we *do* remember is riddled with mondegreens, or misheard lyrics. In these pages you'll find many opportunities to bring a little more completeness and accuracy to your repertoire of rock 'n' roll golden oldies, as well as to rediscover a nearly forgotten gem, wallow in nostalgia, or just browse through some prominent examples of the songwriter's craft.

And if you're still wondering who put the bomp in the bomp ba bomp ba bomp (or, for that matter, who put the ram in the ram-a-lam-a-ding-dong), this is an excellent place to search for likely suspects. All it takes is one sh-boom or do-wah-diddy to place one of these songs in the '50s or early '60s—before rock lyricists, thanks perhaps to the influence of the folk revival, adopted a new sense of artistic and/or political seriousness in the latter half of the '60s. Early rock 'n' roll was giddy with the beat and the explosion of youthful energy, and the wham-bam of the two- or three-minute song form didn't allow much time for lyrical rumination anyway (unless, of course, the subject of the song was a car or motorcycle, which early rock songwriters described lovingly down to the last detail of trim and transmission).

Tear-stained pillows and tragic hot-rod races aside, these songs were created to make you wanna... (Shout!) Kick your heels up and (Shout!) throw your hands up and...

Come on now, say you will.

Contents

Early Rock 'n' Roll

The ABC's of Love

Words and Music by Richard Barrett and Morris Levy

recorded by Frankie Lymon & The Teenagers

Du bop shu-boom,
Bom bom bom bom bom.
Du bop shu-boom,
Bom bom bom bom bom.

I'll always want you,
Because my heart is true.
Come, come, come closer
And I'll tell you of the ABC's.

Darling, believe me,
Ev'ry day my love grows strong.
Find a place there in your heart
And I'll tell you of the ABC's.

Gosh knows I love you,
Heaven knows it's true.
I want to be near you,
J, K, L, M, N, O, P, Q.

Run, honey, and don't be blind.
Sugar, you stay on my mind.
True love is hard to find,
I'll tell you of the ABC's.

You made me love you.
Vow always to be true.
W, X, Y, and Z.
I've told you of the ABC's.

Run, honey, and don't be blind.
Sugar, you stay on my mind.
True love is hard to find,
I'll tell you of the ABC's.

You made me love you.
Vow always to be true.
W, X, Y, and Z.
I've told you of the ABC's.
Told you of the ABC's.

All I Have to Do Is Dream

Words and Music by Boudleaux Bryant

recorded by The Everly Brothers, Richard Chamberlain

Dream, dream, dream, dream.
Dream, dream, dream, dream.

When I want you in my arms,
When I want you and all your charms,
Whenever I want you,
All I have to do is dream,
Dream, dream, dream.

When I feel blue in the night,
And I need you to hold me tight,
Whenever I want you,
All I have to do is dream.

Bridge:
I can make you mine,
Taste your lips of wine,
Anytime, night or day.
Only trouble is, gee whiz,
I'm dreaming my life away.

I need you so that I could die,
I love you so
And that is why
Whenever I want you
All I have to do is dream.

Repeat Bridge and Last Verse

Dream, dream, dream.
Dream, dream, dream, dream.
Dream.

All Shook Up

Words and Music by Otis Blackwell and Elvis Presley

recorded by Elvis Presley

A-well-a bless my soul, what's wrong with me?
I'm itching like a man on a fuzzy tree.
My friends say I'm actin' queer as a bug.

Refrain:
I'm in love.
I'm all shook up!
Mm, mm, oh, oh, yeah!

My hands are shaky and my knees are weak
I can't seem to stand on my own two feet.
Who do you thank when you have such luck?

Please don't ask what's on my mind,
I'm a little mixed up but I feelin' fine.
When I'm near that girl that I love the best,
My heart beats so it scares me to death!
She touched my hand,
What a chill I got,
Her kisses are like a volcano that's hot!
I'm proud to say she's my buttercup,

Refrain

My tongue gets tied when I try to speak,
My insides shake like a leaf on a tree,
There's only one cure for this soul of mine,
That's to have the girl that I love so fine!
She touched my hand,
What a chill I got,
Her kisses are like a volcano that's hot!
I'm proud to say she's my buttercup,

Refrain Three Times

I'm all shook up!

At the Hop

Words and Music by Arthur Singer, John Madara and David White

recorded by Danny & The Juniors

Ba ba ba ba,
Ba ba ba ba,
Ba ba ba ba,
Ba ba ba ba,
At the hop.

Well, you can rock it, you can roll it,
Do the stomp and even stroll it at the hop.
When the records start a-spinnin'
You calypso and you chicken at the hop.
Do the dance sensations that are sweepin' the nation at the hop.

Refrain:
Let's go to the hop!
Let's go to the hop!
(Oh, baby) Let's go to the hop!
(Oh, baby) Let's go to the hop!
Come on, let's go to the hop!

Well, you can swing it, you can groove it,
You can really start to move it at the hop.
Where the jockey is the smoothest
And the music is the coolest at the hop.
All the cats and the chicks can get their kicks at the hop.

Refrain

Baby Love

Words and Music by Brian Holland, Edward Holland and Lamont Dozier

recorded by The Supremes

Baby love, my baby love,
I need you, oh, how I need you.
But all you do is treat me bad,
Break my heart and leave me sad.
Wanna know what did I do wrong
To make you stay away so long.

'Cause baby love, my baby love,
Been missing ya, miss kissing ya.
Instead of breaking up,
Let's start some kissing and making up.
Don't throw our love away.
In my arms why don't you stay?

Baby love, my baby love,
Why must we separate, my love?
All of my whole life through
I never loved no one but you.
Why you do me like you do,
I guess it's me, ooh.

Need to hold you once again, my love,
Feel your warm embrace, my love.
Don't throw our love away,
Please don't do me this way.
Not happy like I used to be,
Loneliness has got the best of me.

My love, my baby love,
I need ya, oh, how I need ya.
Why you do me like you do,
After I've been true to you.
So deep in love with you,
Baby, baby, ooh.

'Til it hurt me, 'til it hurt me.
Ooh, baby love,
Don't throw our love away.
Don't throw our love away.

Barbara Ann

Words and Music by Fred Fassert

recorded by The Regents, The Beach Boys

Refrain:
(Ba, ba, ba, ba, Ba'bra Ann.
Ba, ba, ba, ba, Ba'bra Ann.)
Ba'bra Ann, take my hand.
Ba'bra Ann, you got me rockin' and a-rollin',
Rockin' and a-reelin', Ba'bra Ann,
Ba, ba, ba, Ba'bra Ann.

Went to a dance, lookin' for romance,
Saw Ba'bra Ann, so I thought I'd take a chance.
Oh, Ba'bra Ann, Ba'bra Ann, take my hand.
Oh, Ba'bra Ann, Ba'bra Ann, take my hand.
You got me rockin' and a-rollin',
Rockin' and a-reelin', Ba'bra Ann,
Ba, ba, ba, Ba'bra Ann.

Refrain

Played my fav'rite tune, danced with Betty Lou,
Tried Peggy Sue, but I knew they wouldn't do.
Oh, Ba'bra Ann, Ba'bra Ann, take my hand.
Oh, Ba'bra Ann, Ba'bra Ann, take my hand.
You got me rockin' and a-rollin',
Rockin' and a-reelin', Ba'bra Ann,
Ba, ba, ba, Ba'bra Ann.

Refrain

Be-Bop-A-Lula

Words and Music by Tex Davis and Gene Vincent

recorded by Gene Vincent

Be-bop-a-lula, she's my baby.
Be-bop-a-lula, I don't mean maybe.

Refrain:
Be-bop-a-lula, she's my baby.
Be-bop-a-lula, I don't mean maybe.
Be-bop-a-lula, she's my baby doll,
My baby doll, my baby doll.

She's the gal in the red blue jeans.
She's the queen of all the teens.
She's the one that I know.
She's the one that loves me so.

Refrain

She's the one that's got that beat.
She's the one with the flyin' feet.
She's the one that walks around the store.
She's the one that gets more and more.

Refrain

Be True to Your School

Words and Music by Brian Wilson and Mike Love

recorded by The Beach Boys

When some loud braggart tries to put me down,
And says his school is great,
I tell him right away now what's the matter?
Buddy ain't you heard of my school?
It's number one in the state.

Refrain:
So be true to your school.
Just like you would to your girl or guy.
Be true to your school now,
And let your colors fly.
Be true to your school.

I got a letterman's sweater with the letters in front
I got for football and track.
I'm proud to wear it now,
When I cruise around the other parts of the town.
I got my decal in back.

Refrain

On Friday we'll be jacked up on the football game,
And I'll be ready to fight.
We're gonna smash 'em now.
My girl will be workin' on her pom-poms now,
And she'll be yellin' tonight.

Refrain

So be true to your school.
So be true to your school.

Beechwood 4-5789

Words and Music by Marvin Gaye, William Stevenson and George Gordy

recorded by The Marvelettes

You can have this dance with me.
You can hold my hand
And whisper in my ear sweet words
That I love to hear.
Whisper sweet words in my ear,
Sweet words I love to hear.

Don't be shy, just take your time.
I'd like to get to know you;
I'd like to make you mine.

I've been waiting,
Sitting here so patiently
For you to come over,
Have this dance with me.
And my number is Beechwood 4-5789.
You can call me up and have a date any old time.

Don't be shy, just take your time.
I'd like to get to know you;
I'd like to make you mine.

Beechwood 4-5789.
You can call me up and have a date any old time.
And my number is Beechwood 4-5789.
You can call me up and have a date any old time.

Beep Beep

Words and Music by Carl Ciccetti and Donald Claps

recorded by The Playmates

While riding in my Cadillac, what,
  to my surprise,
A little Nash Rambler was following me,
  about one-third my size.
The guy must have wanted it to pass me up
As he kept on tooting his horn. Beep! Beep!
I'll show him that a Cadillac is not
  a car to scorn.

Refrain:
Beep, beep. (Beep, beep.)
Beep, beep. (Beep, beep.)
His horn went, beep, beep, beep.
  (Beep! Beep!).

I pushed my foot down to the floor to
  give the guy the shake,
But the little Nash Rambler stayed
  right behind; he still had on his brake.
He must have thought his car had more guts
As he kept on tooting his horn. Beep! Beep!
I'll show him that a Cadillac is not
  a car to scorn.

Refrain

My car went into passing gear and
  we took off with dust.
And soon we were doin' ninety,
  must have left him in the dust.
When I peeked in the mirror of my car,
I couldn't believe my eyes.
The little Nash Rambler was right behind,
  you'd think that guy could fly.

Refrain

Now we're doing a hundred and ten,
  it certainly was a race.
For a Rambler to pass a Caddy would
  be a big disgrace.
For the guy who wanted to pass me,
He kept on tooting his horn. Beep! Beep!
I'll show him that a Cadillac is not
  a car to scorn.

Refrain

Now we're doing a hundred and twenty,
  as fast as I could go.
The Rambler pulled alongside of me as
  if I were going slow.
The fellow rolled down his window and
  yelled for me to hear,
"Hey, buddy, how can I get this car out
  of second gear?"

Big Bad John

Words and Music by Jimmy Dean

recorded by Jimmy Dean

Every morning at the mine you could see him arrive,
He stood six-foot-six and weighed two-forty-five.
Kinda broad at the shoulder and narrow at the hip,
And everybody knew you didn't give no lip to Big John!

Refrain:
Big John, Big John,
Big Bad John, Big John.

Nobody seemed to know where John called home,
He just drifted into town and stayed all alone.
He didn't say much, a-kinda quiet and shy,
And if you spoke at all, you just said "hi" to Big John!

Somebody said he came from New Orleans,
Where he got in a fight over a Cajun queen.
And a crashing blow from a huge right hand
Sent a Lousiana fellow to the Promised Land. Big John!

Refrain

Then came the day at the bottom of the mine
When a timber cracked and the men started crying.
Miners were praying and hearts beat fast,
And everybody thought that they'd breathed their last, 'cept John.

Through the dust and the smoke of this man-made hell
Walked a giant of a man that the miners knew well.
Grabbed a sagging timber, gave out with a groan,
And like a giant oak tree, just stood there alone. Big John!

Refrain

And with all of his strength he gave a mighty shove;
Then a miner yelled out, "There's a light up above!"
And twenty men scrambled from a would-be grave,
Now there's only one left down there to save—Big John!

With jacks and timbers they started back down,
Then came that rumble way down in the ground,
And smoke and gas belched out of that mine,
Everybody knew it was the end of the line for Big John!

Refrain

Now they never reopened that worthless pit,
They just placed a marble stand in front of it.
These few words are written on that stand:
"At the bottom of this mine lies a big, big man. Big John!"

Refrain

Big Girls Don't Cry

Words and Music by Bob Crewe and Bob Gaudio

recorded by The 4 Seasons

Big girls don't cry.
Big girls don't cry.

Refrain:
Big girls don't cry, they don't cry.
Big girls don't cry. (Who said they don't cry?)

My girl said good-bye, my, oh my,
My girl didn't cry. (I wonder why.)
(Silly boy) Told my girl we had to break up.
(Silly boy) Thought she would call my bluff.
(Silly boy) Then she said to my surprise,
Big girls don't cry.

Refrain Twice

Baby, I was true, I was true.
Baby, I'm a fool. (I'm such a fool.)
(Silly girl) Shame on you, your mama said.
(Silly girl) You're cryin' in bed.
(Silly girl) Shame on you, you told a lie,
Big girls don't cry.

Big girls don't cry, they don't cry.
Big girls don't cry. (That's just an alibi.)
Big girls don't cry.
Big girls don't cry.

Black Denim Trousers and Motorcycle Boots

Words and Music by Jerry Leiber and Mike Stoller

recorded by The Cheers

Refrain:
He wore black denim trousers and motorcycle boots
And a black leather jacket with an eagle on the back.
He had a hopped-up cycle that took off like a gun.
That fool was the terror of Highway 101.

Well, he never washed his face and he never combed his hair.
He had axle grease embedded underneath his fingernails.
On the muscle of his arm was a red tattoo,
A picture of a heart saying, "Mother, I love you."

He had a pretty girlfriend by the name of Mary Lou,
But he treated her just like he treated all the rest.
And ev'rybody pitied her 'cause ev'rybody knew
He loved that doggone motorcycle best.

Refrain

Mary Lou, poor girl, she pleaded and she begged him not to leave.
She said, "I've got a feeling if you ride tonight I'll grieve."
But her tears were shed in vain, and her ev'ry word was lost
In the rumble of his engine and the smoke from his exhaust.

He took off like a devil, there was fire in his eyes.
He said, "I'll go a thousand miles before the sun can rise."
But he hit a screaming diesel that was California bound,
And when they cleared the wreckage, all they found

Was his black denim trousers and motorcycle boots
And a black leather jacket with an eagle on the back.
But they couldn't find the cycle that took off like a gun,
And they never found the terror of Highway 101.

Blue Suede Shoes

Words and Music by Carl Lee Perkins

recorded by Carl Perkins, Elvis Presley

Well it's one for the money, two for the show,
Three to get ready, now go, cat, go, but

Refrain:
Don't you step on my blue suede shoes.
You can do anything but lay off of my blue suede shoes.

Well, you can knock me down, step on my face,
Slander my name all over the place;
Do anything that you want to do,
But uh-uh, honey, lay off of my shoes.

Refrain

Well, you can burn my house, steal my car,
Drink my cider from an old fruit jar;
Do anything that you want to do,
But uh-uh, honey, lay off of my shoes.

Refrain

Bo Diddley

Words and Music by Ellas McDaniel

recorded by Bo Diddley

Bo Diddley'll buy baby a diamond ring.
If that diamond ring don't shine,
He's gonna take it to a private eye.
If that private eye can't see,
He better not take that ring from me.

Bo Diddley caught a nanny goat
To make his pretty baby a Sunday coat.
Bo Diddley caught a bearcat,
To make his pretty baby a Sunday hat.

Won't you come to my house and rack that bone,
Take my baby all the way from home.
Look at that bodo, oh, where's he been,
Up your house and gone again.

Bo Diddley, Bo Diddley, have you heard,
My pretty baby said she was a bird.

Bobby's Girl

Words and Music by Gary Klein and Henry Hoffman

recorded by Marcie Blane

When people ask of me,
What would you like to be
Now that you're not a kid anymore?
I know just what to say,
I answer right away,
There's just one thing I've been wishing for.

Refrain:
I wanna be Bobby's girl,
I wanna be Bobby's girl.
That's the most important thing to me.
And if I was Bobby's girl,
If I was Bobby's girl,
What a faithful, thankful girl I'd be.

Each night I sit at home,
Hoping that he will phone,
But I know Bobby has someone else.
Still in my heart I pray
There soon will come a day
When I will have him all to myself.

Refrain

Book of Love

Words and Music by Warren Davis, George Malone and Charles Patrick

recorded by The Monotones

Tell me, tell me, tell me,
Oh, who wrote the book of love?
I've got to know the answer;
Was it someone from above?

Refrain:
I wonder, wonder who, who,
Who wrote the book of love?

I love you, darling,
Baby, you know I do.
I've got to see this book of love,
Find out why it's true.

Refrain

Chapter one says to love her,
To love her with all your heart.
Chapter two you tell her
You're never, never, never, never ever gonna part.
In chapter three remember
The meaning of romance.
In chapter four you break up,
But you give her just one more chance.

Refrain

Baby, baby, baby,
I love you, yes, I do.
Well, it says so in this book of love,
Ours is the one that's true.

Refrain

A Boy Without a Girl

Words and Music by Sidney Jacobson and Ruth Sexter

recorded by Frankie Avalon

A boy without a girl
Is a song without a tune,
Is a year without a June, my love.
A boy without a girl
Is a day without a night,
Is a star without a light, my love.

And since you've come to me,
All the world has come to shine,
'Cause I've found girl who's really mine.
And if you stay with me,
All your life you'll never be
A girl without a boy, my love.

Bread and Butter

Words and Music by Larry Parks and Jay Turnbow

recorded by The Newbeats

I like bread and butter,
I like toast and jam.
That's what my baby feeds me.
I'm her lovin' man.
He likes bread and butter.
He likes toast and jam.
That's what his baby feeds him.
He's her loving man.

She don't cook mashed potatoes,
Don't cook T-bone steak.
Don't feed me peanut butter,
She knows that I can't take
No more bread and butter,
No more toast and jam.
That's what his baby feeds him.
He found his baby eatin' with some other man.

Got home early one mornin',
Much to my surprise,
She was eating chicken and dumplings
With some other guy.
No more bread and butter,
No more toast and jam,
I found my baby eating
With some other man.

Breaking Up Is Hard to Do

Words and Music by Howard Greenfield and Neil Sedaka

recorded by Neil Sedaka

You tell me that you're leaving,
I can't believe it's true.
Girl, there's just no living without you.

Don't take your love away from me.
Don't you leave my heart in misery.
If you go then I'll be blue,
Breaking up is hard to do.

Remember when you held me tight,
And you kissed me all through the night.
Think of all that we've been through,
Breaking up is hard to do.

They say that breaking up is hard to do.
Now I know, I know that it's true.
Don't say that this is the end.
Instead of breaking up,
I wish that we were making up again,
We were making up again.

I beg of you, don't say good-bye;
Can't we give our love a brand new try?
Yeah, come on, babe, let's start anew,
'Cause breaking up is hard to do.

Bye Bye, Love

Words and Music by Felice Bryant and Boudleaux Bryant

recorded by The Everly Brothers

There goes my baby
With someone new.
She sure looks happy;
I sure am blue.
She was my baby
Till he stepped in.
Good-bye to romance
That might have been.

Refrain:
Bye bye, love.
Bye bye, happiness.
Hello loneliness.
I think I'm gonna cry.
Bye bye, love.
Bye bye, sweet caress.
Hello emptiness.
I feel like I could die.
Bye bye, my love, good-bye.

I'm through with romance,
I'm through with love.
I'm through with counting
The stars above.
And here's the reason
That I'm so free,
My loving baby
Is through with me.

Refrain

Calendar Girl

Words and Music by Howard Greenfield and Neil Sedaka

recorded by Neil Sedaka

I love, I love, I love my calender girl.
Yeah, sweet calender girl.
I love, I love, I love my calender girl,
Each and ev'ry day of the year.

(January) You start the year off fine.
(February) You're my little Valentine.
(March) I'm gonna march you down the aisle,
(April) You're the Easter bunny when you smile.

Refrain:
Yeah, yeah, my heart's in a whirl.
I love, I love, I love my little calender girl.
Ev'ry day, ev'ry day of the year.

(May) Maybe if I ask your dad and mom,
(June) They'll let me take you to the junior prom.
(July) Like a firecracker I'm aglow.
(August) When you're on the beach you steal the show.

Refrain

(September) I'll light the candles at your sweet sixteen.
(October) Romeo and Juliet on Halloween.
(November) I'll give thanks that you belong to me.
(December) You're the present 'neath my Christmas tree.

Refrain

Can't Help Falling in Love

Words and Music by George David Weiss, Hugo Peretti and Luigi Creatore

from the Paramount Picture *Blue Hawaii*
recorded by Elvis Presley

Wise men say only fools rush in,
But I can't help falling in love with you.
Shall I stay?
Would it be a sin?
If I can't help falling in love with you.

Like a river flows,
Surely to the sea.
Darling so it goes,
Some things are meant to be.

Take my hand, take my whole life too,
For I can't help falling in love in with you.
For I can't help falling in love with you.

Cathy's Clown

Words and Music by Don Everly

recorded by The Everly Brothers

Refrain:
Don't want your love anymore.
Don't want your kisses, that's for sure.
I die each time I hear this sound.
Here he comes; that's Cathy's clown.

I've got to stand tall.
You know a man can't crawl.
For when he knows you tell lies
And he lets them pass by,
Then he's not a man at all.

Refrain

When you see me shed a tear,
And you know that it's sincere.
Don't you think it's kind of sad
That you're treating me so bad,
Or don't you even care?

Refrain

That's Cathy's clown.
That's Cathy's clown.

Chains

Words and Music by Gerry Goffin and Carole King

recorded by The Cookies, The Beatles

Chains, my baby's got me locked up in chains,
And they ain't the kind that you can see.
Wo, these chains of love got a hold on me, yeah.

Chains, well I can't break away from these chains.
Can't run around, 'cause I'm not free.
Wo, these chains of love won't let me be, yeah.

Chains, my baby's got me locked up in chains,
And they ain't the kind that you can see.
Wo, these chains of love got a hold on me, yeah.
I wanna tell you, pretty baby, I think you're fine.
I'd like to love you, but darling I'm imprisoned by these:

Chains, my baby's got me locked up in chains,
And they ain't the kind that you can see.
Wo, these chains of love got a hold on me, yeah.
Please believe me when I tell you, your lips are sweet.
I'd like to kiss them, but I can't break away from all of these:

Chains, my baby's got me locked up in chains,
And they ain't the kind that you can see.
Wo, these chains of love got a hold on me, yeah.
Chains, chains of love.

Chains of Love

Words and Music by A. Nugetre and Harry Vanwalls

recorded by Pat Boone

Chains of love have tied my heart to you.
Chains of love have made me feel so blue.
Well, now I'm your prisoner;
Tell me what you're gonna do.

Are you gonna leave me,
Are you gonna make me cry?
Are you gonna leave me,
Are you gonna make me cry?
These chains are gonna haunt me
Until the day I die.

Well, if you're gonna leave me,
Please, won't you set me free?
Well, if you're gonna leave me,
Please, won't you set me free?
I can't bear these chains that bind me
Unless you're here with me.

Well, it's three o'clock in the mornin',
The moon is shinin' bright.
Yes, it's three o'clock in the mornin',
The moon is shinin' bright.
I just sit and wonder,
Where can you be tonight?

Chantilly Lace

Words and Music by J.P. Richardson

recorded by Big Bopper

Chantilly lace
And a pretty face
And a pony tail
Hangin' down,
Wiggle in her walk
And a giggle in her talk,
Makes the world go 'round.

Ain't nothin' in this world
Like a big-eyed girl
To make me act so funny,
Make me spend my money,
Make me feel real loose
Like a long-necked goose,
Like a girl.

Spoken:
Oh, baby,
That's-a what I like.

Charlie Brown

Words and Music by Jerry Leiber and Mike Stoller

recorded by The Coasters

Fee fee fi fi fo fo fum,
I smell smoke in the auditorium.

Refrain:
Charlie Brown, Charlie Brown,
He's a clown, that Charlie Brown.
He's gonna get caught, just you wait and see.
"Why is ev'rybody always pickin' on me?"

That's him on his knees, I know that's him,
Yellin' "Seven come eleven" down in the boys' gym.

Refrain

Who's always writin' on the walls?
Who's always goofin' in the halls?
Who's always throwin' spitballs?
Guess who? "Who, me?" Yeah, you!

Who walks in the classroom cool and slow?
Who calls the English teacher daddy-o?

Refrain

Crying

Words and Music by Roy Orbison and Joe Melson

recorded by Roy Orbison

I was alright for a while
I could smile for a while
But I saw you last night,
You held my hand real tight
As you stopped to say "hello."
Oh, you wished me well,
You couldn't tell,
That I'd been crying over you.
Crying over you.
When you said, "So long"
Left me standing all alone,
Alone and crying,
Crying, crying, crying.
It's hard to understand,
But the touch of your hand
Can start me crying.

I thought that I was over you,
But it's true, so true;
I love you even more than I did before.
But darling, what can I do?
For you don't love me
And I'll always be
Crying over you,
Crying over you.
Yes, now you're gone,
And from this moment on,
I'll be crying
Crying, crying, crying.
It's hard to understand,
But the touch of your hand
Can start me crying,
Yeah, crying, crying over you.

Crying in the Rain

Words and Music by Carole King and Howard Greenfield

recorded by The Everly Brothers

I'll never let you see
The way my broken heart is hurtin' me.
I've got my pride and I know how to hide
All my sorrow and pain.
I'll do my crying in the rain.

If I wait for cloudy skies,
You won't know the rain from the tears in my eyes.
You'll never know that I still love you.
So, though the heartaches remain,
I'll do my crying in the rain.

Raindrops fallin' from heaven
Could never wash away my misery.
But since we're not together,
I look for stormy weather
To hide the tears I hope you'll never see.

Someday when my crying's done
I'm gonna wear a smile and walk in the sun.
I may be a fool,
But till then, darling, you'll never see me complain.
I'll do my crying in the rain.
I'll do my crying in the rain.

Dancing in the Street

Words and Music by Marvin Gaye, Ivy Hunter and William Stevenson

recorded by Martha & The Vandellas

Calling out around the world,
Are you ready for a brand new beat?
Summer's here and the time is right
For dancing in the street.
They're dancing in Chicago,
Down in New Orleans,
In New York City.

Refrain:
All we need is music, sweet music.
There'll be music everywhere.
There'll be swinging and swaying and
    records playing,
Dancing in the street.
Oh, it doesn't matter what you wear,
Just as long as you are there.
So come on, ev'ry guy, grab a girl.
Ev'rywhere around the world
They'll be dancing. (Dancing in the street.)
They're dancing in the street.
    (Dancing in the street.)

It's an invitation across the nation,
A chance for folks to meet.
There'll be laughing, singing, and music
    swinging,
Dancing in the street.
Philadelphia, P.A.
Baltimore and D.C. now.
Can't forget the Motor City.

Refrain

Way down in L.A. ev'ry day,
They're dancing in the street.
(Dancing in the street.)
Let's form a big, strong line, get in time,
We're dancing in the street.
(Dancing in the street.)
Across the ocean blue, me and you,
We're dancing in the street.
(Dancing in the street.)

Dead Man's Curve

Words and Music by Jan Berry, Roger Christian, Brian Wilson and Art Kornfeld

recorded by Jan & Dean

I was cruisin' in my Sting Ray late one night,
When an XKE pulled up on my right.
He rolled down the window of his shiny new Jag,
Challenged me then and there to a drag.
I said, "You're on, buddy, my mill's runnin' fine.
Let's come off the line now at Sunset and Vine.
But I'll go you one better if you got the nerve.
Let's race all the way to Dead Man's Curve."

Refrain:
Dead Man's Curve, it's no place to play.
Dead Man's Curve, you must keep away.
Dead Man's Curve, I can hear 'em say,
"Won't come back from Dead Man's Curve."

The street was deserted late Friday night.
We were buggin' each other while we sat at the light.
We both popped the clutch when the light turned green.
You shoulda heard the whine from my screamin' machine.
I flew past La Brea, Schwab's, and Crescent Heights,
And all the Jag could see were my six tail lights.
He passed me at Doheny an' I started to swerve,
But I pulled her out and there I was at Dead Man's Curve.

Dead Man's Curve.
Dead Man's Curve.

Spoken:
Well, the last thing I remember, Doc, I started to swerve.
Then I saw the Jag slide into the curve.
I know I'll never forget that horrible sight.
I guess I found out for myself that everyone was right.

Sung:
Won't come back from Dead Man's Curve.

Refrain

© 1963 (Renewed 1991) SCREEN GEMS-EMI MUSIC INC.

Devil or Angel

Words and Music by Blanche Carter

recorded by Bobby Vee

Devil or angel, I can't make up my mind.
Which one you are, I'd like to wake up and find.
Devil or angel, dear, whichever you are,
I miss you, I miss you, I miss you.

Devil or angel, please say you'll be mine.
Love me or leave me, I'll go out of my mind.
Devil or angel, dear, whichever you are,
I need you, I need you, I need you.

You look like an angel,
Your smile is so divine.
But you keep me guessing,
Will you ever be mine?

Devil or angel, please say you'll be mine.
Love me or leave me, I've made up my mind.
Devil or angel, dear, whichever you are,
I love you, I love you, I love you.

Devoted to You

Words and Music by Boudleaux Bryant

recorded by The Everly Brothers

Darling, you can count on me
Till the sun dries up the sea.
Until then I'll always be
Devoted to you.

I'll be yours through endless time,
I'll adore your charms sublime.
Guess by now you know that I'm
Devoted to you.

I'll never hurt you, I'll never lie,
I'll never be untrue.
I'll never give you reason to cry,
I'd be unhappy if you were blue.

Through the years my love will grow,
Like a river it will flow.
It can't die because I'm so
Devoted to you.

The Diary

Words and Music by Howard Greenfield and Neil Sedaka

recorded by Neil Sedaka

How I'd like to look into that little book,
The one that has the lock and key,
And know the boy that you care for,
The boy who's in your diary.

When it's late at night, what is the name you write?
Oh, what I'd give if I could see.
Am I the boy that you care for,
The boy who's in your diary?

Do you recall and make note of all
The little things I say and do?
The name you underline, I'm hoping that it's mine.
Darling, I'm so in love with you.

Please don't leave me blue. Make all my dreams come true.
You know how much you mean to me.
Say I'm the boy that you care for,
The boy who's in your diary.

Do Wah Diddy Diddy

Words and Music by Jeff Barry and Ellie Greenwich

recorded by Manfred Mann

There he was, just a-walkin' down the street, singin'
Do wah diddy diddy down diddy do.
Poppin' his fingers and a-shuffling his feet, singin'
Do wah diddy diddy down diddy do.
He looked good (yeah, yeah).
He looked fine (yeah, yeah).
He looked good, he looked fine,
And I nearly lost my mind.

Before I knew it he was walkin' next to me, singin'
Do wah diddy diddy down diddy do.
He took my hand, just as nat'ral as can be, singin'
Do wah diddy diddy down diddy do.
We walked on (yeah, yeah)
To my door (yeah, yeah).
We walked on to my door,
And he stayed a little more.

My, my, my, my,
I knew we were fallin' in love.
My, my, my, my,
I told him all the things I was dreamin' of.

Now we're together nearly ev'ry single day, singin'
Do wah diddy diddy down diddy do.
We're so happy, and that's how we're gonna stay, singin'
Do wah diddy diddy down diddy do.

'Cause I'm his (yeah, yeah),
And he's mine (yeah, yeah).
Well, I'm his and he's mine,
And the weddin' bells will chime, singin'
Do wah diddy diddy down diddy do.
Do wah diddy diddy down diddy do.

Don't

Words and Music by Jerry Leiber and Mike Stoller

recorded by Elvis Presley

Don't, don't, that's what you say
Each time that I hold you this way.
When I feel like this and I want to kiss you,
Baby, don't say don't.

Don't, don't leave my embrace,
For here in my arms is your place.
When the night grows cold and I want to hold you,
Baby, don't say don't.

If you think that this is just a game I'm playing,
If you think that I don't mean ev'ry word I'm saying,
Don't, don't, don't feel that way.
I'm your love and yours I will stay.

This you can believe;
I will never leave you,
Heaven knows I won't.
Baby, don't say don't.

Don't Be Cruel (To a Heart That's True)

Words and Music by Otis Blackwell and Elvis Presley

recorded by Elvis Presley

Don't be cruel to a heart that's true.
Don't be cruel to a heart that's true.
I don't want no other love.
Baby, it's just you I'm thinking of.

You known I can be found
Sitting all alone.
If you can't come around,
At least please telephone.
Don't be cruel to a heart that's true.

Baby, if I made you mad
For something I might have said,
Please, let's forget the past
'Cause the future looks bright ahead.
Don't be cruel to a heart that's true.

I don't want no other love,
Baby, it's just you I'm thinking of.
Well don't stop thinkin' of me.
Don't make me feel this way.
Come on over here and love me.
You know I wanna say
Don't be cruel to a heart that's true.

Why should we be apart?
I really, really love you,
Baby, cross my heart.
Let's walk up to the preacher
And let us say, "I do."
And then you'll know you have me,
And I'll know I have you too.

Don't be cruel to a heart that's true.
Why should we be apart?
I don't want no other love.
Baby, it's just you I'm thinking of.

Don't Worry Baby

Words and Music by Brian Wilson and Roger Christian

recorded by The Beach Boys

Well, it's been buildin' up inside of me
For oh, I don't know how long.
I don't know why, but I keep thinkin'
Something's bound to go wrong.
But she looks in my eyes
And makes me realize
When she says,

Refrain:
"Don't worry baby,
Ev'rything will work out all right.
Don't worry, baby."

I guess I shoulda kept my mouth shut
When I started to brag about my car.
But I can't back down now
Because I pushed the other guys too far.
She makes me come alive
And makes me wanna drive
When she says,

Refrain

She said, "Now, baby, when you race today,
Just take along my love with you.
And if you knew how much I loved you,
Baby, nothing could go wrong with you."
Oh, what she does to me
When she makes love to me
And she says,

Refrain

Dream Baby (How Long Must I Dream)

Words and Music by Cindy Walker

recorded by Roy Orbison

Dream baby got me dreamin'
Sweet dreams the whole day through.
Dream baby got me dreamin'
Sweet dreams night time too.
I love you and I'm dreamin' of you.
That won't do.
Dream baby, make me stop my dreamin'.
You can make my dreams come true.

Sweet dream baby,
Sweet dream baby,
Sweet dream baby,
How long must I dream?

Dream Lover

Words and Music by Bobby Darin

recorded by Bobby Darin

Ev'ry night I hope and pray
A dream lover will come my way,
A girl to hold in my arms
And know the magic of her charms.
Because I want a girl to call my own,
I want a dream lover so I don't have to dream alone.

Dream lover, where are you,
With a love, oh, so true
And I hand that can hold
To feel you near when I grow old?
Because I want a girl to call my own,
I want a dream lover so I don't have to dream alone.

Someday, I don't know how,
I hope you'll hear my plea.
Some way, I don't know how,
She'll bring her love to me.

Dream lover, until then,
I'll go to sleep and dream again.
That's the only thing to do
Until my lover's dreams come true.
Because I want a girl to call my own,
I want a dream lover so I don't have to dream alone.

Earth Angel

Words and Music by Jesse Belvin

recorded by The Crew-Cuts, The Penguins

Earth angel, earth angel,
Will you be mine,
My darling, dear, love you all the time.
I'm just a fool, a fool in love with you.

Earth Angel, earth angel,
The one I adore, love you forever and evermore.
I'm just a fool, a fool in love with you.

I fell for you,
And I knew the vision of your love's loveliness,
I hope and I pray
That someday I'll be the vision of your happiness.

Earth angel, earth angel,
Please be mine, my darling dear, love you all the time.
I'm just a fool, a fool in love with you.

Ev'rybody's Somebody's Fool
(Everybody's Somebody's Fool)

Words and Music by Jack Keller and Howard Greenfield

recorded by Connie Francis

The tears I cried for you could fill an ocean,
But you don't know how many tears I cry;
And though you only lead me on and hurt me,
I couldn't bring myself to say goodbye.

Refrain:
'Cause ev'rybody's somebody's fool,
Ev'rybody's somebody's plaything,
And there are no exceptions to the rule.
Yes, everybody's somebody's fool.

I told myself it's best that I forget you,
Though I'm a fool at least I know the score;
But, darling, I'd be twice as blue without you.
It hurts, but I'd come running back for more.

Refrain

Some day you'll find someone to really care for,
And if her love should prove to be untrue,
You'll know how much this heart of mine is breaking,
You'll cry for her the way I cried for you. Yes...

Refrain

Everyday

Words and Music by Norman Petty and Charles Hardin

recorded by Buddy Holly

Ev'ry day it's a-getting closer,
Going faster than a roller coaster.
Love like yours will truly come my way.

Ev'ry day it's a-getting faster,
Ev'ryone said, "Go on up and ask her."
Love like yours will truly come my way.

Ev'ry day seems a little longer.
Ev'ry way love's a little stronger.
Come what may,
Do you ever long for true love from me?

Ev'ry day it's a-getting closer,
Going faster than a roller coaster.
Love like yours will truly come my way.

Fun, Fun, Fun

Words and Music by Brian Wilson and Mike Love

recorded by The Beach Boys

Well, she got her daddy's car
And she cruised through the hamburger
    stand now.
Seems she forgot all about the library
Like she told her old man now.
And with her radio blastin',
Goes cruising just as fast as she can now.

Refrain:
And she'll have fun, fun, fun,
Till her daddy takes the T-bird away.

Well, the girls can't stand her
'Cause she walks, looks, and drives like an
    ace now.
She makes the Indy 500
Look like a Roman chariot race now.
A lotta guys try to catch her,
But she leads them on a wild goose chase
    now.

Refrain

A-well, you knew all along
That your dad was gettin' wise to you now.
And since he took your set of keys
You've been thinking that your fun is all
    through now.
But you can come along with me,
'Cause we gotta lotta things to do now.

Three Times:
And you'll have fun, fun, fun,
Now that daddy took the T-bird away.

Fun, fun, fun,
Now that daddy took the T-bird away.

Get a Job

Words and Music by Earl Beal, Richard Lewis, Raymond Edwards and William Horton

recorded by The Silhouettes

Refrain:
Sha da da da, sha da da da da,
Sha da da da, sha da da da da,
Sha da da da, sha da da da da,
Yip yip yip yip yip yip yip yip,
Mum mum mum mum mum mum.
Get a job, sha da da da, sha da da da da.

Ev'ry morning about this time
She get me out of my bed,
A-crying, get a job.
After breakfast ev'ry day
She throws the want ads right my way
And never fails to say,
Get a job, sha da da da, sha da da da da.

Refrain

And when I get the paper,
I read it through and through,
And my girl never fails to say
If there is any work for me.
And when I go back to the house,
I hear the woman's mouth
Preaching and a-crying,
Tell me that I'm lying
'Bout a job that I never could find.

Refrain

Sha da da da, sha da da da da,
Sha da da da, sha da da da da,
Sha da da da, sha da da da da.

Go Away, Little Girl

Words and Music by Gerry Goffin and Carole King

recorded by Steve Lawrence

Go away, little girl,
Go away, little girl,
I'm not supposed to be alone with you.
I know that your lips are sweet,
But our lips must never meet.
I belong to someone else and I must be true.

Oh, go away, little girl,
Go away, little girl.
It's hurting me more each minute that you delay.
When you are near me like this,
You're much too hard to resist.
So go away, little girl,
Before I beg you to stay.

Repeat Song

Good Luck Charm

Words and Music by Aaron Schroeder and Wally Gold

recorded by Elvis Presley

Don't want a four leaf clover;
Don't want an old horse shoe.
Want your kiss 'cause I just can't miss
With a good luck charm like you.

Refrain:
Come on and be my little good luck charm.
Uh-huh-huh, you sweet delight.
I want a good luck charm a-hangin' on my arm
To have, to hold, to hold tonight.

Don't want a silver dollar,
Rabbit's foot on a string.
The happiness in your warm caress
No rabbit's foot can bring.

Refrain

If I found a lucky penny,
I'd toss it across the bay.
Your love is worth all the gold on earth;
No wonder that I say,

Refrain

Goodnight My Love, Pleasant Dreams

Words and Music by George Motola and John Marascalco

recorded by The McGuire Sisters

Goodnight, my love,
Pleasant dreams and sleep tight, my love.
May tomorrow be sunny and bright
And bring you closer to me.

Before you go
Please remember I need you so,
And this love I have for you
Will never grow cold.

If you should awake in the still of the night,
Please have no fear.
Just close your eyes, then you'll realize
That my love will watch over you, dear, always.

Repeat Verse 1

Great Balls of Fire

Words and Music by Otis Blackwell and Jack Hammer

recorded by Jerry Lee Lewis

You shake my nerves and you rattle my brain.
Too much love drives a man insane.
You broke my will,
But what a thrill.
Goodness gracious, great balls of fire!

I laughed at love 'cause I thought it was funny.
You came along and you moved me, honey.
I changed my mind,
Love's just fine.
Goodness gracious, great balls of fire!

Kiss me, baby.
Woo, it feels good.
Hold me, baby.
Girl just let me love you like a lover should.
You're fine, so kind,
I'm gonna tell the world that you're mine, mine, mine.

I chew my nails and I twiddle my thumb.
I'm nervous but it sure is fun.
Come on, baby, you're driving me crazy.
Goodness gracious, great balls of fire.

The Great Pretender

Words and Music by Buck Ram

recorded by The Platters

Oh, yes I'm the great pretender,
Pretendin' I'm doin' well;
My need is such, I pretend too much,
I'm lonely but no one can tell.

Oh yes, I'm the great pretender,
Adrift in a world of my own;
I play the game but, to my real shame,
You've left me to dream alone,
Too real is this feeling of make believe,
Too real when I feel what my heart can't conceal;
Oh, yes, I'm the great pretender,
Just laughin' and gay like a clown;
I seem to be what I'm not, you see,
I'm wearin' my heart like a crown;
Pretendin' that you're still aroun'.

The Green Door

Words and Music by Bob Davie and Marvin Moore

recorded by Jim Lowe

Midnight, one more night without sleepin',
Watching till the morning comes peepin',
Green door, what's the secret you're keepin'?
There's an old piano, and they play it hot
Behind the green door.
Don't know what they're doin', but they laugh a lot
Behind the green door.
Wish they'd let me in so I could find out what's
Behind the green door.

Knocked once, tried to tell 'em I'd been there.
Door slammed, hospitality's thin there.
Wonder just what's goin' on in there.
Saw an eyeball peepin' through a smoky cloud
Behind the green door.
When I said Joe sent me, someone laughed out loud
Behind the green door.
All I want to do is join the happy crew
Behind the green door.

Greenfields

Words and Music by Terry Gilkyson, Richard Dehr and Frank Miller

recorded by The Brothers Four

Once there were greenfields kissed by the sun;
Once there were valleys where rivers used to run;
Once there was blue sky with white clouds high above;
Once they were part of an everlasting love.
We were the lovers who strolled through greenfields.

Greenfields are gone now, parched by the sun;
Gone from the valleys where rivers used to run;
Gone with the cold wind that swept into my heart;
Gone with the lovers who let their dreams depart.
Where are the greenfields that we used to roam?

I'll never know what made you run away.
How can I keep searching when dark clouds hide the day?
I only know there's nothing here for me,
Nothing in this wide world left for me to see.

But I'll keep on waitin' 'til you return.
I'll keep on waiting until the day you learn
You can't be happy while your heart's on the roam.
You can't be happy until you bring it home,
Home to the greenfields and me once again.

Happy Birthday Sweet Sixteen

Words and Music by Howard Greenfield and Neil Sedaka

recorded by Neil Sedaka

Tonight's the night I've waited for,
Because you're not a baby anymore.
You've turned into the prettiest girl I've ever seen.
Happy birthday sweet sixteen.

What happened to that funny face?
My little tomboy now wears satins and lace.
I can't believe my eyes; you're just a teenage dream.
Happy birthday sweet sixteen.

If I should smile with sweet surprise,
It's just that you've grown up before my very eyes,
You've turned into the prettiest girl I've ever seen.
Happy birthday sweet sixteen.

When you were only six, I was your big brother;
Then when you were ten, we didn't like each other.
When you were thirteen, you were my funny valentine.
But since you've grown up your future is sewn up,
From now on, you're gonna be mine.

Repeat Song

Happy, Happy Birthday Baby

Words and Music by Margo Sylvia and Gilbert Lopez

recorded by The Tune Weavers

Happy, happy birthday baby.
Although you're with somebody new,
Thought I'd drop a line to say
That I wish this happy day
Would find me beside you.

Happy, happy birthday baby.
No, I can't call you my baby.
Seems like years ago we met
On a day I can't forget,
'Cause that's when we fell in love.

Do you remember the names we had for each other?
You were my pretty, I was your baby.
How could we say good-bye?

Hope I didn't spoil your birthday.
I know I'm acting kind of crazy,
So I'll close this note to you
With good luck and wishes too.
Happy, happy birthday baby.

Do you remember the names we had for each other?
You were my pretty, I was your baby.
How could we say good-bye?

Hope I didn't spoil your birthday.
I know I'm acting kind of crazy,
So I'll close this note to you
With good luck and wishes too.
Happy, happy birthday baby.

He'll Have to Go

Words and Music by Joe Allison and Audrey Allison

recorded by Jim Reeves

Put your sweet lips a little closer to the phone.
Let's pretend that we're together all alone.
I'll tell the man to turn the jukebox way down low.
And you can tell your friend there with you he'll have to go.

Whisper to me, tell me do you love me true
Or is he holding you the way I do?
Though love is blind, make up your mind, I've got to know.
Should I hang up or will you tell him he'll have to go?

You can't say the words I want to hear
While you're with another man.
If you want me, answer "yes" or "no,"
Darling, I will understand.

Repeat Verse 1

He's a Rebel

Words and Music by Gene Pitney

recorded by The Crystals

See the way he walks down the street.
Watch the way he shuffles his feet.
My, how he holds his head high
When he goes walking by.
He's my guy!

When he holds my hand I'm so proud,
'Cause he's not just one of the crowd.
My baby's always the one to try
The things they've never done.
And just because of that they say:

He's a rebel, and he'll never ever be any good,
He's a rebel, 'cause he never ever does what he should.
Well, just because he doesn't do what ev'rybody else does,
That's no reason why I can't give him all my love.
He is always good to me, always treats me tenderly,
'Cause he's not a rebel, no, no, no,
He's not a rebel, no, no, no, to me.

If they don't like him that way,
They won't like me after today.
I'll be standing right by his side when they say:

He's a rebel, and he'll never ever be any good,
He's a rebel, 'cause he never ever does what he should.
Well, just because he doesn't do what ev'rybody else does,
That's no reason why we can't share a love.
He is always good to me, good to him I'll try to be,
'Cause he's not a rebel, no, no, no,
He's not a rebel, no, no, no, to me.

Heartbreak Hotel

Words and Music by Mae Boren Axton, Tommy Durden and Elvis Presley

recorded by Elvis Presley

Well, since my baby left me,
Well I found a new place to dwell,
Down at the end of Lonely Street,
At Heartbreak Hotel.
I'm so lonely,
I'm so lonely,
I'm so lonely that I could die.

And though it's overcrowded
You can still find some room
For broken hearted lovers
To cry there in the gloom,
And be so lonely,

Oh, so lonely,
Oh, so lonely they could die.

The bell hop's tears are flowing,
The clerk's dressed in black.
They've been so long in Lonely Street
They never will go back.
And they're so lonely,
Oh, they're so lonely,
They're so lonely they pray to die.

So if your baby leaves you
And you have a tale to tell,
Just take a walk down Lonely Street
To Heartbreak Hotel
Where you'll be so lonely,
And I'll be so lonely,
We'll be so lonely
That we could die.

Heatwave (Love Is Like a Heatwave)

Words and Music by Edward Holland, Lamont Dozier and Brian Holland

recorded by Martha & The Vandellas

Whenever I'm with him
Something inside
Starts to burnin'
And I'm filled with desire.
Could it be
A devil in me?
Or is this the way
Love's supposed to be?

Refrain:
It's like a heatwave
Burnin' in my heart.
I can't keep from cryin'
It's tearin' me apart.

Whenever he calls my name
Soft, low, sweet and plain,
I feel, yeah, yeah,
Well I feel that burnin' flame.
Has high blood pressure
Got a hold on me
Or is this the way
Love's supposed to be?

Refrain

Sometimes I stare into space,
Tears all over my face.
I can't explain it, don't understand it.
I ain't never felt like this before.
Now that funny feelin'

Has me amazed.
I don't know what to do,
My head's in a haze.

Refrain

Yeah, yeah, yeah, yeah, yeah,
Yeah, whoa ho.
Yeah, yeah, yeah,
Yeah ho.
Don't pass up this chance,
This time it's true romance.

Refrain

Hello Mary Lou

Words and Music by Gene Pitney and C. Mangiaracina

recorded by Ricky Nelson

You passed me by one sunny day,
Flashed those big brown eyes my way,
And oo I wanted you forever more.
I'm not one that gets around,
I swear my feet stuck to the ground,
And though I never did meet you before,

Refrain:
I said, "Hello Mary Lou, good-bye heart.
Sweet Mary Lou, I'm so in love with you.
I knew, Mary Lou, we'd never part.
So hello Mary Lou, good-bye heart."

I saw your lips, I heard your voice,
Believe me I just had no choice.
Wild horses couldn't make me stay away.
I thought about a moonlit night,
My arms about you good an' tight,
That's all I had to see for me to say,

Refrain

Hey Paula

Words and Music by Ray Hildebrand

recorded by Paul & Paula

He:
Hey! Hey! Paula, I wanna marry you.
Hey! Hey! Paula, no one else will ever do.
I've waited so long for school to be through.
Paula, I can't wait no more for you, my love, my love.

She:
Hey! Paul, I've been waiting for you.
Hey! Hey! Hey! Paul, I wanna marry you too.
If you love me true, if you love me still.
Our love will always be real, my love, my love.

Refrain (Both):
True love means planning a life for two,
Being together the whole day through.
True love means waiting and hoping that soon
Wishes we've made will come true, my love, my love.

He:
Hey! Hey! Paula, I wanna marry you.

She:
Hey! Hey! Paul, I want to marry you too.

Refrain (Both)

Hey There Lonely Girl (Hey There Lonely Boy)

Words and Music by Earl Shuman and Leon Carr

recorded by Ruby & The Romantics

Refrain:
Hey there, lonely girl, lonely girl,
Let me make your broken heart like new.
Hey there, lonely girl, lonely girl,
Don't you know this lonely boy loves you?

Ever since he broke your heart, you seem so lost
Each time you pass my way.
Oh, how I long to take your hand and say don't cry,
I'll kiss your tears away.

Refrain

You think that only his two lips can kiss your lips
And make your heart stand still,
But once you're in my arms you'll see
No one can kiss your lips the way I will.

Refrain

Hey there, lonely girl, lonely girl,
Don't you know this lonely boy loves you?

Honeycomb

Words and Music by Bob Merrill

recorded by Jimmie Rodgers

Honeycomb, honeycomb.

Refrain:
Honeycomb, won't ya be my baby?
Honeycomb, be my own.
Just a hank of hair and a piece of bone
Made a walkin', talkin' honeycomb.
Honeycomb, won't ya be my baby?
Honeycomb, be my own.
What a darn good life
When I've got a wife like honeycomb.

It's a darn good life and it's kinda funny
How the bee was made and the bee made the honey,
The honeybee, lookin' for a home,
Made my honeycomb.
Then they roamed the world and they gathered all
Of the honeycomb into one sweet ball.
The honeycomb from a million trips
Made my baby's lips.

Refrain

Now have you heard tell how they made a bee,
Then tried a hand at a green, green tree?
So the tree was made and I guess you've heard,
Next they made a bird.
Then they went around lookin' everywhere,
Takin' love from here and from there,
And they stored it up in a little cart,
For my honey's heart.

Refrain

Hound Dog

Words and Music by Jerry Leiber and Mike Stoller

recorded by Elvis Presley

You ain't nothin' but a hound dog,
Cryin' all the time.
You ain't nothin' but a hound dog,
Cryin' all the time.
Well, you ain't never caught a rabbit
And you ain't no friend of mine.

When they said you was high-classed,
Well, that was just a lie.
When they said you was high-classed,
Well, that was just a lie.
Well, you ain't never caught a rabbit
And you ain't no friend of mine.

Hushabye

Words and Music by Doc Pomus and Mort Shuman

Recorded by The Mystics

Hushabye, hushabye,
Oh my darlin', don't you cry.
Guardian angels up above
Take care of the one I love.
Ooh, ooh.
Ooh, ooh.

Pillows lying on your bed;
Oh, my darling, rest your head.
Sandman will be coming soon,
Singing you a slumber tune.
Ooh, ooh.
Ooh.

Lullaby and goodnight,
In your dreams I'll hold you tight.
Lullaby and goodnight,
Till the dawn's early light.

Repeat Verse 1

I Almost Lost My Mind

Words and Music by Ivory Joe Hunter

recorded by Pat Boone

When I lost my baby,
I almost lost my mind.
When I lost my baby,
I almost lost my mind.
My head is in a spin
Since she left me behind.

I pass a million people,
I can't tell who I meet.
I pass a million people,
I can't tell who I meet,
'Cause my eyes are full of tears.
Where can my baby be?

I went to see a gypsy
And had my fortune read.
I went to see a gypsy
And had my fortune read.
I hung my head in sorrow
When she said what she said.

I can tell you, people,
The news was not so good.
Well, I can tell you, people,
The news was not so good.
She said, "Your baby has quit you.
This time she's gone for good."

I Can't Stop Loving You

Words and Music by Don Gibson

recorded by Ray Charles

Those happy hours that we once knew,
Though long ago, still make me blue.
They say that time heals a broken heart,
But time has stood still since we've been apart.

I can't stop loving you,
So I've made up my mind
To live in memory
Of old lonesome times.
I can't stop wanting you,
It's useless to say,
So I'll just live my life
In dreams of yesterday.

Repeat Verse 1

I can't stop loving you,
There's no use to try.
Pretend there's someone new;
I can't live a lie.
I can't stop wanting you
The way that I do.
There's only been one love for me,
That one love is you.

I Get Around

Words and Music by Brian Wilson and Mike Love

recorded by The Beach Boys

Refrain:
I get around from town to town
I'm a real cool head,
I'm makin' real good bread.

I'm gettin' bugged, drivin' up an' down the same ol' strip.
I gotta find a new place where the kids are hip.
My buddies and me are gettin' real well known,
Yeah, the bad guys know us and they leave us alone.

Refrain

We always take my car 'cause it's never been beat.
And we've never missed yet with the girls we meet.
None of the guys go steady 'cause it wouldn't be right,
To leave your best girl home on a Saturday night.

Repeat Refrain and Fade

I Got a Woman

Words and Music by Ray Charles

recorded by Jimmy McGriff

I got a woman way over town,
She's good to me, oh yeah!
Well, I got a woman way over town,
She's good to me, oh yeah!
Now she's my dreamboat, oh, yes indeed,
She's just the kind of girl I need.
I found a woman way over town,
She's good to me, oh yeah!

I save my kisses and all my huggin'
Just for her, oh yeah!
I save my kisses and all my huggin'
Just for her, oh yeah!
When I say, "Baby, please take my hand,"
She holds me tight, she's my lover girl.
I found a woman way over town,
She's good to me, oh yeah!

She always answers my beck and call,
Ever-lovin' mama mama tree-top tall.
I feel so proud walkin' by her side,
Couldn't get a better girl,
No matter how hard I tried.

I got a woman way over town,
She's good to me, oh yeah!
Someday we'll marry, way over town,
She's good to me, oh yeah!
Someday we'll marry, don't you understand,
'Cause she's my only lover girl.
I found a woman way over town,
She's good to me, oh yeah!

I Got Stung

Words and Music by Aaron Schroeder and David Hill

recorded by Elvis Presley

Holy smoke, a-land sakes alive!
I never thought this could happen to me.

Mm, yeah! Mm, yeah!
I got stung by a sweet honey bee.
Oh, what a feeling come over me.
It started in my eyes,
Crept up to my head,
Flew to my heart
Till I was stung dead.
I'm done, uh-uh, I got stung!

Mm, yeah! Mm, yeah!
She had all that I wanted and more,
And I've seen honey bees before.
Started buzzin' in my ear,
Buzzin' in my brain.
Got stung all over
But I feel no pain.
I'm done, uh-uh, I got stung!

Now, don't think I'm complainin'.
I'm mighty pleased we met,
'Cause you gimme just one little peck
On the back of my neck
And I break out in a cold, cold sweat.

If I live to a hundred and two,
I won't let nobody sting me but you.
I'll be buzzin' 'round your hive
Ev'ry day at five,
And I'm never gonna leave once I arrive
'Cause I'm done, uh-uh, I got stung!

('Til) I Kissed You

Words and Music by Don Everly

recorded by The Everly Brothers

Never felt like this until I kissed you.
How did I exist until I kissed you?
Never had you on my mind;
Now you're there all the time.
Never knew what I missed until I kissed you.
Uh-huh, I kissed you, oh yeah.

Things have really changed since I kissed you.
My life's not the same now that I kissed you.
Mmm, you got a way about you;
Now I can't live without you.
Never knew what I missed until I kissed you.
Uh-huh, I kissed you, oh yeah.

You don't realize what you do to me.
And I didn't realize what a kiss could be.
Mmm, you got a way about you;
Now I can't live without you.
Never knew what I missed until I kissed you.
Uh-huh, I kissed you,
Oh yeah, I kissed you.

I Love How You Love Me

Words and Music by Barry Mann and Larry Kolber

recorded by The Paris Sisters

I love how you love me.
I love how you kiss me.
And when I'm away from you,
I love how you miss me.
And I love the way
You always treat me tenderly.
But, darling, most of all,
I love how you love me.

I love how your heart beats
Whenever I hold you.
I love how you think of me
Without being told to.
And I love the way your touch
Is almost heavenly.
But, darling, most of all,
I love how you love me.

Repeat Verse 2

I love how you love me.
I love how you love me.
I love how you love me.

I Walk the Line

Words and Music by John R. Cash

recorded by Johnny Cash

I keep a close watch on this heart of mine.
I keep my eyes wide open all the time.
I keep the ends out for the tie that binds.
Because you're mine,
I walk the line.

I find it very, very easy to be true.
I find myself alone when each day is through.
Yes, I'll admit that I'm a fool for you.
Because you're mine,
I walk the line.

As sure as night is dark and day is light,
I keep you on my mind both day and night.
And happiness I've known proves that it's right.
Because you're mine,
I walk the line.

You've got a way to keep me on your side.
You give me a cause for love that I can't hide.
For you I know I'd even try to turn the tide.
Because you're mine,
I walk the line.

I keep a close watch on this heart of mine.
I keep my eyes wide open all of the time.
I keep the ends out for the tie that binds.
Because you're mine,
I walk the line.

I Want You, I Need You, I Love You

Words by Maurice Mysels
Music by Ira Kosloff

recorded by Elvis Presley

Hold me close, hold me tight;
Make me thrill with delight.
Let me know where I stand from the start.
I want you, I need you, I love you with all my heart.

Ev'ry time that you're near
All my cares disappear.
Darling, you're all that I'm livin' for.
I want you, I need you, I love you more and more.

I thought I could live without romance
Before you came to me,
But now I know that I will go
On loving you eternally.

Won't you please be my own?
Never leave me alone,
'Cause I die ev'ry time we're apart.
I want you, I need you, I love you with all my heart.

I'm Stickin' with You

Words and Music by Dave Alldred, James Bowen, Buddy Knox and Donnie Lanier

recorded by Jimmy Bowen

Refrain:
Be bop, I love you, baby.
Be bop, I don't mean maybe.
Be bop, I love you, baby.
I'm stickin' with you.
I'm stickin' with you.

Years may come and a-go.
I will love you so.
No matter where we go,
I'm stickin' with you.
I'm stickin' with you.

New loves may come your way,
But my love's here to stay.
This is why I say,

Refrain

New loves may come your way,
But my love's here to stay.
This is why I say,

Refrain

In the Still of the Nite (I'll Remember)

Words and Music by Fred Parris

recorded by The Five Satins

(Shoo doop doo be doo,
Shoo doop shoo be doo,
Shoo doop shoo be doo.
Shoo doop shoo be wah.)

In the still of the nite
I held you, held you tight.
Oh, I love, love you so,
Promise I'll never let you go
In the still of the nite.
(In the still of the nite.)

I remember that nite in May
That the stars were bright up above.
I'll hope and I'll pray
To keep your precious love.

So, before the light,
Hold me again with all of your might
In the still of the nite.
(In the still of the nite.)

(Shoo wop shoo wah,
Shoo wop shoo wah,
Shoo wop shoo wah,
Shoo wop shoo wah.)

So before the light,
Hold me again
With all of your might
In the still of the nite.

(In the still of the nite.)

In the still of the nite.
(Shoo doop shoo be doo,
Shoo doop shoo be doo,
Shoo doop shoo be doo,
Shoo doop shoo be wah.)…

It's My Party

Words and Music by Herb Wiener, Wally Gold and John Gluck, Jr.

recorded by Lesley Gore

Nobody knows where my Johnny has gone,
But Judy left the same time.
Why was he holding her hand,
When he's supposed to be mine?

Refrain:
It's my party and I'll cry if I want to,
Cry if I want to,
Cry if I want to.
You would cry too, if it happened to you.

Play all my records, keep dancing all night,
But leave me alone for awhile.
'Til Johnny's dancing with me,
I've got no reason to smile.

Refrain

Judy and Johnny just walked through the door,
Like a queen and her king.
Oh, what a birthday surprise,
Judy's wearing his ring.

Refrain

It's Now or Never

Words and Music by Aaron Schroeder and Wally Gold

recorded by Elvis Presley

Refrain:
It's now or never
Come hold me tight.
Kiss me, my darlin'
Be mine tonight.
Tomorrow will be too late.
It's now or never,
My love won't wait.

When I first saw you
With your smile so tender,
My heart was captured
My soul surrendered.
I've spent a lifetime
Waiting for the right time.
Now that you're near
The time is here at last.

Refrain

Just like a willow
We could cry an ocean,
If we lost true love
And sweet devotion.
Your lips excite me
Let your arms invite me.
For who knows when
We'll meet again this way.

Refrain

It's Only Make Believe

Words and Music by Conway Twitty and Jack Nance

recorded by Conway Twitty

People see us everywhere, they think you really care,
But myself I can't deceive, I know it's only make believe.
My one and only prayer, is that someday you'll care.

My hopes, my dreams come true, my one and only you,
No one will ever know, how much I love you so,
My only prayer will be, someday you'll care for me,
But it's only make believe.

My hopes, my dreams come true, my life I'd give for you,
My heart, a wedding ring, my all, my everything.
My heart I can't control, you rule my very soul,
My plans, my hopes, my schemes, you are my everything,
But it's only make believe.

My one and only prayer is that someday you'll care,
My hopes, my dreams come true, my one and only you.
No one will ever know, just how much I love you so,
My only prayer will be that someday you'll care for me
But it's only make believe.

It's So Easy

Words and Music by Buddy Holly and Norman Petty

recorded by The Crickets

Refrain:
It's so easy to fall in love.
It's so easy to fall in love.

People tell me love's for fools,
So here I go breaking all the rules.
It seems so easy, so dog-gone easy;
It seems so easy where you're concerned.
My heart has learned.

Refrain

Look into your heart and see
What your love book has set apart for me.
It seems so easy, so dog-gone easy;
It seems so easy where you're concerned.
My heart has learned.

Refrain

Jailhouse Rock

Words and Music by Jerry Leiber and Mike Stoller

recorded by Elvis Presley

The warden threw a party in the county jail.
The prison band was there and they began
  to wail.
The band was jumpin' and the joint began
  to swing.
You should've heard those knocked-out
  jailbirds sing.

Refrain:
Let's rock!
Everybody, let's rock!
Everybody in the whole cell block
Was a-dancin' to the Jailhouse Rock.
Spider Murphy played the tenor saxophone.
Little Joe was blowin' on the slide trombone.
The drummer boy from Illinois went crash,
  boom, bang:
The whole rhythm section was the
  Purple Gang.

Refrain
Number Forty-Seven said to Number Three:
You're the cutest little jailbird I ever did see.
I sure would be delighted with your
  company.
Come on and do the Jailhouse Rock with me.

Refrain

The sad sack was a-sittin' on a block of
  stone,
Way over in the corner weeping all alone.
The warden said: "Hey buddy, don't you be
  no square.
If you can't find a partner use a wooden
  chair!"

Refrain

Shifty Henry said to Bugs: "For heaven's
  sake,
No one's lookin'; now's our chance to make
  a break."
Bugsy turned to Shifty and he said: "Nix, nix;
I wanna stick around awhile and get my
  kicks."

Refrain

James (Hold the Ladder Steady)

Words and Music by John D. Loudermilk

recorded by Sue Thompson

James and I, we went to Mama
And showed her my diamond ring.
She said, "My poor little baby, you must be crazy
To think of such a thing."

Refrain:
So James, James, hold the ladder steady.
James, James, I'm packed and I am ready.
James, James, hold the ladder steady.
I'm a-comin' down to your arms.
I'm a-comin' down to your arms.

James and I, we went to Daddy
And said, "Dad, we want to be wed."
Dad said, "Nope, you'll just have to elope!"
And laughed as he went to bed.

Refrain

I'd hate to see 'em in the morning
When they both completely flip!
He'll be saying, "They can't!" She'll be feelin' faint.
And I'll be kissin' my husband's lips.

Refrain

Kansas City

Words and Music by Jerry Leiber and Mike Stoller

recorded by Wilbert Harrison, The Beatles

I'm goin' to Kansas City, Kansas City here I come.
I'm goin' to Kansas City, Kansas City here I come.
They got a crazy way of lovin' there and I'm gonna get me some.

I'm gonna be standin' on the corner Twelfth Street and Vine.
I'm gonna be standin' on the corner Twelfth Street and Vine,
With my Kansas City baby and a bottle of Kansas City wine.
Well, I might take a train, I might take a plane,
But if I have to walk, I'm goin' just the same.

Refrain:
I'm goin' to Kansas City, Kansas City here I come.
They got a crazy way of lovin' there and I'm gonna get me some.

I'm goin' to pack my clothes, leave at the crack of dawn.
I'm goin' to pack my clothes, leave at the crack of dawn.
My old lady will be sleepin', she won't know where I'm gone.
'Cause if I stay with that woman, I know I'm gonna die.
Gotta find a brand-new baby, and that's the reason why.

Refrain

Last Kiss

Words and Music by Wayne Cochran

recorded by J. Frank Wilson

Refrain:
Well, oh where, oh, where can my baby be?
The Lord took her away from me.
She's gone to heaven so I got to be good,
So I can see my baby when I leave this world.

We were out on a date in my daddy's car.
We hadn't driven very far.
There in the road straight ahead
A car was stalled, the engine was dead.
I couldn't stop so I swerved to the right.
I'll never forget the sound that night.
The cryin' tires, the bustin' glass,
The painful scream that I heard last.

Refrain

When I woke up, the rain was pouring down.
There was people standin' all around.
Something warm was runnin' in my eyes,
But I found my baby somehow that night.
I raised her head until she smiled and said,
"Hold me, darling, for a little while."
I held her close and kissed her our last kiss.
I found her love that I knew I had missed.
But now she's gone even though I hold her tight.
I lost my love, my life, that night.

Refrain

Let the Good Times Roll

Words and Music by Sam Theard and Fleecie Moore

recorded by Shirley & Lee

Refrain:
Come on, baby, let the good times roll.
Come on, baby, let me thrill your soul.
Come on, baby, let the good times roll.
Roll on and on.

Come on, baby, let me hold you tight.
Tell me ev'rything is right tonight.
Come on, baby, let the good times roll.
Roll on and on.

Come on, baby, gonna have a ball.
Come on, baby, put your troubles up against
   the wall.
Come on, baby, let the good times roll.
Roll on and on.

Come on, baby, let us paint the town.
Come on, baby, don't let nothin' ever bring
   us down.
Come on, baby, let the good times roll.
Roll on and on.

Feel so good in my arms,
Sugar baby, you're my good luck charm.

Refrain

Let's go, baby, on a crazy fling.
Love can be such a swingin' thing.
Come on, baby, let the good times roll.
Roll on and on.

Feel so good when you're close,
Sugar baby, I dig you the most.

Refrain

Limbo Rock

Words and Music by Billy Strange and Jon Sheldon

recorded by Chubby Checker

Ev'ry limbo boy and girl
All around the limbo world
Gonna do the limbo rock
All around the limbo clock.

Refrain:
Jack be limber, Jack be quick,
Jack go under limbo stick.
All around the limbo clock,
Hey, let's do the limbo rock.

Spoken:
Limbo lower now,
Limbo lower now.
How low can you go?

First, you spread your limbo feet,
Then you move to limbo beat.
Limbo ankle, limbo knee;
Bend back like a limbo tree.

Refrain

Get yourself a limbo girl,
Give that chick a limbo whirl.
There's a limbo moon above.
You will fall in limbo love.

Refrain

Spoken:
Don't move that limbo bar.
You'll be a limbo star.
How low can you go?

Lipstick on Your Collar

Words by Edna Lewis
Music by George Goehring

recorded by Connie Francis

When you left me all alone at the record hop,
Told me you were goin' out for a soda pop,
You were gone for quite a while,
Half an hour or more.
You came back and man, oh man,
This is what I saw.

Refrain:
Lipstick on your collar told a tale on you.
Lipstick on your collar said you were untrue.
Bet your bottom dollar you and I are through,
'Cause lipstick on your collar told a tale on you.

You said it belonged to me; made me stop and think.
Then I noticed yours was red, mine was baby pink.
Who walked in but Mary Jane, lipstick all a mess.
Were you smoochin' my best friend? Guess the answer's yes.

Refrain

Little Deuce Coupe

Music by Brian Wilson
Words by Roger Christian

recorded by The Beach Boys

Well, I'm not braggin', babe, so don't put me down,
But I've got the fastest set of wheels in town.
When something comes up to me, it don't even try,
'Cause if it had a set of wings, man, I know she could fly.

Refrain:
She's my little deuce coupe.
You don't know what I got.

Just a little deuce coupe with a flat-head mill,
But she'll walk a Thunderbird like she's standin' still.
She's ported and relieved and she's stroked and she's bored.
She'll do a hundred and forty with the top end floored.

Refrain

She's got a competition clutch with the four on the floor, yeah.
She purrs like a kitten till the lake pipes roar.
And if that ain't enough to make you flip your lid,
There's one more thing, I've got the pink slip, daddy!

And comin' off the line when the light turns green,
She blows 'em outta the water like you've never seen.
I get pushed out of shape, and it's hard to steer,
When I get rubber in all four gears.

Refrain

Repeat Verses 3 and 4

Refrain

The Little Old Lady (From Pasadena)

Words and Music by Don Altfeld and Roger Christian

recorded by Jan & Dean

The little old lady from Pasadena
(Go Granny, go Granny, go Granny go)
Has a pretty little flower bed of white gardenias.
(Go Granny, go Granny, go Granny go)
But parked in a rickety old garage,
There's a brand new shiny red super-stocked Dodge.

Refrain:
And ev'rybody's sayin' that there's nobody meaner
Than the little old lady from Pasadena.
She drives real fast and she drives real hard.
She's the terror of Colorado Boulevard.
It's the little old lady from Pasadena!

If you see her on the strip don't try to choose her.
(Go Granny, go Granny, go Granny go)
You might have a goer, but you'll never lose her.
(Go Granny, go Granny, go Granny go)
She's gonna get a ticket now, sooner or later,
'Cause she can't keep her foot off the accelerator.

Refrain

You'll see her all the time, just gettin' her kicks now,
(Go Granny, go Granny, go Granny go)
With her four-speed stick and a four-two-six now.
(Go Granny, go Granny, go Granny go)
The guys come to race her from miles around,
But she'll give 'em a length, then she'll shut 'em down.

Refrain

The Loco-Motion

Words and Music by Gerry Goffin and Carole King

recorded by Little Eva

Everybody's doin' a brand new dance now.
(C'mon, baby, do the Locomotion.)
I know you'll get to like it if you give it a chance now.
(C'mon, baby, do the Locomotion.)
My little baby sister can do it with ease,
Its easier than learnin' your A-B-C's.
So come on, come on, do the Locomotion with me.
You gotta swing your hips now.
Come on, baby, jump up, jump back.
Oh, well, I think you got the knack.

Now that you can do it, let's make a chain now.
(C'mon, baby, do the Locomotion.)
A chug-a chug-a motion like a railroad train now.
(C'mon, baby, do the Locomotion.)
Do it nice and easy now, don't lose control,
A little bit of rhythm and a lot of soul.
Come on, come on and do the Locomotion with me.
(C'mon, baby, do the Locomotion.)

Move around the floor in a locomotion.
(C'mon, baby, do the Locomotion.)
Do it holdin' hands if you get the notion.
(C'mon, baby, do the Locomotion.)
There's never been a dance that's so easy to do.
It even makes you happy when you're feelin' blue.
So, come on, come on, do the Locomotion with me.
(C'mon, baby, do the Locomotion.)
(C'mon, baby, do the Locomotion.)

Lollipop

Words and Music by Beverly Ross and Julius Dixon

recorded by The Chordettes

Refrain
Lollipop, lollipop,
Oh, lolli, lolli, lolli,
Lollipop, lollipop,
Oh, lolli, lolli, lolli,
Lollipop, lollipop,
Oh, lolli, lolli, lolli,
Lollipop.

Call my baby lollipop, tell you why,
Her kiss is sweeter than an apple pie.
And when she does her shaky rockin' dance,
Man, I haven't got a chance.
I call her

Refrain

Sweeter than candy on a stick,
Huckleberry, cherry, or lime.
If you had a choice, she'd be your pick,
But lollipop is mine.
Oh,

Refrain

Crazy way she thrills-a me, tell you why,
Just like-a lightning from the sky.
She loves to kiss me till I can't see straight.
Gee, my lollipop is great.
I call her

Refrain

Lonely Teardrops

Words and Music by Berry Gordy, Gwen Gordy Fuqua and Tyran Carlo

recorded by Jackie Wilson

Lonely teardrops, my pillow's never dry.
Lonely teardrops, come home, come home.
Just say you will, say you will, say you will.
Hey, hey, my heart is cryin', cryin'.

Lonely teardrops, my pillow's never dry.
Lonely teardrops, come home, come home.
Just say you will, say you will, say you will.
Hey, hey.

Just give me another chance for our romance.
Come on and tell me that one day you'll return,
'Cause ev'ry day that you've been gone away,
You'll know how my heart does nothing but burn.

Cryin' lonely teardrops, my pillow's never dry.
Lonely teardrops, come home, come home.
Just say you will, say you will, say you will.
Hey, hey, hey, say it right now, baby.
Come on, come on.

Love Me

Words and Music by Jerry Leiber and Mike Stoller

recorded by Elvis Presley

Treat me like a fool,
Treat me mean and cruel,
But love me.
Break my faithful heart,
Tear it all apart,
But love me.
If you ever go,
Darling, I'll be, oh, so lonely.
I'll be sad and blue,
Crying over you, dear, only.

I would beg and steal
Just to feel your heart
Beating close to mine.
Ev'ry night I pray
To the stars that shine
Above me,
Beggin' on my knees,
All I ask is please,
Please, love me.

Love Me Tender

Words and Music by Elvis Presley and Vera Matson

recorded by Elvis Presley

Love me tender, love me sweet;
Never let me go.
You have made my life complete,
And I love you so.

Refrain:
Love me tender, love me true
All my dreams fulfill.
For, my darlin', I love you,
And I always will.

Love me tender, love me long;
Take me to your heart.
For it's there that I belong,
And we'll never part.

Refrain

Love me tender, love me dear;
Tell me you are mine.
I'll be yours through all the years,
Till the end of time.

Refrain

Love Potion Number 9

Words and Music by Jerry Leiber and Mike Stoller

recorded by The Clovers, The Searchers

I took my troubles down to Madame Ruth.
You know, that gypsy with the gold-capped tooth.
She's got a storefront down on Thirty-Fourth and Vine,
Sellin' little bottles of Love Potion Number Nine.

I told her that I was a flop with chicks.
I've been that way since 1956.
She looked at my palm and she made a magic sign.
She said, "What you need is Love Potion Number Nine."

She bent down and turned around and gave me a wink.
She said, "I'm gonna mix it up right here in the sink."
It smelled like turpentine and looked like India ink.
I held my nose, I closed my eyes, I took a drink.

I didn't know if it was day or night.
I started kissin' ev'rything in sight.
But when I kissed a cop down at Thirty-Fourth and Vine,
He broke my little bottle of Love Potion Number Nine.

Loving You

Words and Music by Jerry Leiber and Mike Stoller

recorded by Elvis Presley

I will spend my whole life through
Loving you, loving you.
Winter, summer, springtime, too,
Loving you, loving you.
Makes no diff'rence where I go or what I do.
You know that I'll always be loving you.

If I'm seen with someone new,
Don't be blue, don't be blue.
I'll be faithful, I'll be true,
Always true, true to you.
There is only one for me, and you know who.
You know that I'll always be loving you.

Lucille

Words and Music by Richard Penniman and Albert Collins

recorded by Little Richard

Lucille, won't you do your sister's will?
Oh, Lucille, won't you do your sister's will?
Well, you ran away and left. I love you still.

Lucille, please come back where you belong.
Oh, Lucille, please come back where you belong.
I been good to you, baby. Please don't leave me alone.

Lucille, baby, satisfy my heart.
Oh, Lucille, baby, satisfy my heart.
I slaved for you, baby, and gave you such a wonderful start.

I woke up this morning, Lucille was not in sight.
I asked my friends about her, but all their lips were tight.

Lucille, please come back where you belong.
I been good to you, baby. Please don't leave me alone.

Make the World Go Away

Words and Music by Hank Cochran

recorded by Eddy Arnold

Do you remember when you loved me
Before the world took me astray?
If you do, then forgive me
And make the world go away.

Refrain:
Make the world go away
And get it off my shoulders.
Say the things you used to say
And make the world go away.

I'm sorry if I hurt you.
I'll make it up day by day.
Just say you love me like you used to
And make the world go away.

Refrain

Maybe Baby

By Norman Petty and Charles Hardin

recorded by The Crickets

Maybe, baby, I'll have you.
Maybe, baby, you'll be true.
Maybe, baby, I'll have you for me.

It's funny, honey, you don't care.
You never listen to my prayer.
Maybe, baby, you will love me someday.

Well, you are the one that makes me sad,
And you are the one that makes me glad.
When someday you want me
I'll be there. Just wait and see.

Maybe, baby, I'll have you.
Maybe, baby, you'll be true.
Maybe, baby, I'll have you for me.

Moments to Remember

Words by Al Stillman
Music by Robert Allen

recorded by The Four Lads

The New Year's Eve we did the town,
The day we tore the goalpost down,
We will have these moments to remember.

The quiet walks, the noisy fun,
The ballroom prize we almost won,
We will have these moments to remember.

Though summer turns to winter
And the present disappears,
The laughter we were glad to share
Will echo through the years.

When other nights and other days
May find us gone our sep'rate ways,
We will have these moments to remember.

My Boy Lollipop

Words and Music by Morris Levy and Johnny Roberts

recorded by Millie Small

My boy lollipop,
You made my heart go giddy up.
You are as sweet as candy;
You're my sugar dandy.
Ho, ho, my boy lollipop,
Never ever leave me,
Because it would grieve me;
My heart told me so.

I love ya, I love ya, I love ya so,
That I want ya to know.
I need ya, I need ya, I need ya so,
And I'll never let you go.

My boy lollipop,
You make my heart go giddy up.
You set my world on fire.
You are my one desire.
My boy lollipop.
My boy lollipop.

My Boyfriend's Back

Words and Music by Robert Feldman, Gerald Goldstein and Richard Gottehrer

recorded by The Angels

My boyfriend's back and you're gonna be in
trouble.
(Hey, la-di-la, my boyfriend's back.)
When you see him comin', better cut on the
double.
(Hey, la-di-la, my boyfriend's back.)
You've been spreading lies that I was untrue.
(Hey, la-di-la, my boyfriend's back.)
So look out now 'cause he's comin' after
you.
(Hey, la-di-la, my boyfriend's back.)
And he knows that you've been tryin',
And he knows that you've been lyin'.

He's been gone for such a long time.
(Hey, la-di-la, my boyfriend's back.)
Now he's back and things will be fine.
(Hey, la-di-la, my boyfriend's back.)
You're gonna be sorry you were ever born.
(Hey, la-di-la, my boyfriend's back.)
'Cause he's kinda big and he's awful strong.
(Hey, la-di-la, my boyfriend's back.)
And he knows about your cheatin',
Now you're gonna get a beatin'.

What made you think he'd believe all your
lies?
(Ah-oo, ah-oo.)
You're a big man now, but he'll cut you
down to size!
(Ah-oo.)
Wait and see!

My boyfriend's back, he's gonna save my
reputation.
(Hey, la-di-la, my boyfriend's back.)
If I were you, I'd take a permanent vacation.
(Hey, la-di-la, my boyfriend's back.)
La-di-la, my boyfriend's back!
La-di-la, my boyfriend's back!

My Guy

Words and Music by William "Smokey" Robinson

recorded by Mary Wells

Nothing you could say can tear me away from my guy.
Nothing you could do 'cause I'm stuck like glue to my guy.
I'm sticking to my guy like a stamp to a letter.
Like birds of a feather, we stick together.
I can tell you from the start
I can't be torn apart
From my guy.

Nothing you could do could make me untrue to my guy.
Nothing you could buy could make me tell a lie to my guy.
I gave my guy my word of honor.
To be faithful and I'm gonna.
You best be believing,
I won't be deceiving
My guy.

As a matter of opinion I think he's tops.
My opinion is he's the cream of the crop.
As a matter of taste to be exact,
He's my ideal as a matter of fact.

No muscle-bound man could take my hand from my guy.
No handsome face could ever take the place of my guy.
He may not be a movie star,
But when it comes to being happy, we are.
There's not a man today
Who could take me away
From my guy.

My Heart Is an Open Book

Lyric by Hal David
Music by Lee Pockriss

recorded by Carl Dobkins, Jr.

Refrain:
Look! Look! My heart is an open book.
I love nobody but you.
Look! Look! My heart is an open book.
My love is honest and true.

Some jealous so-and-so wants us to part.
That's why he's tellin' you that I've got a cheatin' heart.
Don't believe all those lies.
Darlin', just believe your eyes and
Look! Look! My heart is an open book.
I love nobody but you.

No Particular Place to Go

Words and Music by Chuck Berry

recorded by Chuck Berry

Riding along in my automobile,
My baby beside me at the wheel.
I stole a kiss at the turn of a mile,
My curiosity running wild.
Cruising and playing the radio,
With no particular place to go.

Riding along in my automobile,
I was anxious to tell her the way I feel.
So I told her softy and sincere,
And she leaned and whispered in my ear.
Cuddling more and driving slow,
With no particular place to go.

No particular place to go,
So we parked way out on the cocamo.
The night was young and the moon was gold,
So we both decided to take a stroll.
Can you imagine the way I felt?
I couldn't unfasten her seat belt.

Riding along in my calaboose,
Still trying to get her belt unloose.
All the way home I held a grudge,
For the safety belt that wouldn't budge.
Cruising and playing the radio,
With no particular place to go.

Oh Boy!

Words and Music by Sunny West, Bill Tilghman and Norman Petty

recorded by The Crickets

Refrain:
All of my love, all of my kissin',
You're gonna see what you been missin', oh boy!
When you're with me, oh boy!
The world can see that you were meant for me.

All of my life I been waitin',
Tonight there'll be no hesitatin', oh boy!
When you're with me, oh boy!
The world can see that you were meant for me.

Oh, can't you hear my poor heart callin',
Stars appear and shadows fall.
A little bit o' lovin' makes ev'rything right.
I'm gonna have some fun tonight!

Refrain

Oh! Carol

Words and Music by Howard Greenfield and Neil Sedaka

recorded by Neil Sedaka

Oh! Carol, I am but a fool.
Darling, I love you, though you treat me cruel.
You hurt me and you make me cry.
But if you leave me I will surely die.

Darling, there will never be another
'Cause I love you so.
Don't ever leave me. Say you'll never go.
I will always want you for my sweetheart,
No matter what you do.
Oh, oh, oh, Carol, I'm so in love with you.

Oh, Lonesome Me

Words and Music by Don Gibson

recorded by Don Gibson

Ev'rybody's goin' out and havin' fun.
I'm just a fool for stayin' home and havin' none.
I can't get over how she set me free.
Oh, lonesome me.

A bad mistake I'm makin' by just hangin' round.
I know that I should have some fun and paint the town.
A lovesick fool that's blind and just can't see.
Oh, lonesome me.

I'll bet she's not like me.
She's out and fancy free,
Flirting with the boys with all her charms.
But I still love her so,
And, brother, don't you know,
I'd welcome her right back here in my arms.

Well, there must be some way I can lose these lonesome blues.
Forget about the past and find somebody new.
I've thought of everything from A to Z.
Oh, lonesome me.

Oh, Pretty Woman

Words and Music by Roy Orbison and Bill Dees

recorded by Roy Orbison

Pretty woman,
Walking down the street,
Pretty woman,
The kind I like to meet,
Pretty woman.
I don't believe you, you're not the truth.
No one could look as good as you.

Pretty woman,
Won't you pardon me,
Pretty woman,
I couldn't help but see,
Pretty woman,
That you look lovely as can be.
Are you lonely just like me?

Pretty woman, stop awhile,
Pretty woman, talk awhile,
Pretty woman, give your smile to me.
Pretty woman, yeah, yeah, yeah.

Pretty woman, look my way,
Pretty woman, say you'll stay with me.
'Cause I need you, I'll treat you right.
Come with me, baby.
Be mine tonight.

Pretty woman,
Don't walk on by,
Pretty woman,
Don't make me cry,
Pretty woman, don't walk away.
Hey, O.K.
If that's the way it must be, O.K.

I guess I'll go on home, it's late.
There'll be tomorrow night, but wait!
What do I see?
Is she walking back to me?
Yeah, she's walking back to me!
Oh, pretty woman.

On Broadway

Words and Music by Barry Mann, Cynthia Weil, Mike Stoller and Jerry Leiber

recorded by The Drifters

They say the neon lights are bright
On Broadway;
They say there's always magic in the air;
But when you're walkin' down the street,
And you ain't had enough to eat,
The glitter rubs right off and you're nowhere.

They say the women treat you fine
On Broadway;
But lookin' at them just gives me the blues;
'Cause how ya gonna make some time,
When all you got is one thin dime,
And one thin dime won't even shine your shoes.

They say that I won't last too long
On Broadway;
I'll catch a Greyhound bus for home, they say;
But they're dead wrong, I know they are.
'Cause I can play this here guitar,
And I won't quit till I'm a star on Broadway.

One Fine Day

Words and Music by Gerry Goffin and Carole King

recorded by The Chiffons

One fine day you'll look at me,
And you will know our love was meant to be.
One fine day
You're gonna want me for your girl.

The arms I long for
Will open wide,
And you'll be proud
To have me walking by your side.
One fine day
You're gonna want me for your girl.

Though I know you're the kind of boy
Who only wants to run around.
I'll keep waiting and someday, darling,
You'll come to me when you want to settle down, oh.

One fine day
We'll meet once more,
And then you'll want the love you threw away before.
One fine day,
You're gonna want me for your girl.

One fine day,
Oh, oh,
One fine day,
You're gonna want me for your girl.
Shoo-be-do-be-do-be-do-be-do wah...

Only the Lonely (Know the Way I Feel)

Words and Music by Roy Orbison and Joe Melson

recorded by Roy Orbison

Only the lonely know the way I feel tonight.
Only the lonely know this feeling ain't right.
There goes my baby, there goes my heart.
They're gone forever, so far apart.
But only the lonely know why I cry.
Only the lonely.

Only the lonely know the heartaches I've been through.
Only the lonely know I cry and cry for you.
Maybe tomorrow a new romance,
No more sorrow, but that's the chance
You got to take if you're lonely, heartbreak.
Only the lonely.

Palisades Park

Words and Music by Chuck Barris

recorded by Freddy Cannon

Last night I took a walk after dark,
A swingin' place called Palisades Park;
To have some fun and see what I could see,
That's where the girls are.
I took a ride on the shoot-the-chute.
The girl I sat beside was awful cute.
And when we stopped
She was holdin' hands with me.

My heart was flyin' up like a rocket ship,
Down a-like a roller coaster,
Fast a-like a loop-the-loop,
And around a-like a merry-go-round.

We ate and ate at a hot dog stand,
We danced around to a rockin' band;
And when I could, I gave that girl a hug,
In the tunnel of love.

You'll never know how great a kiss can feel,
When you've stopped at the top of the Ferris wheel,
Where I fell in love, down at Palisades Park.

Party Doll

Words and Music by James Bowen and Buddy Knox

recorded by Buddy Knox with the Rhythm Orchids

Well, all I want is a party doll
To come along with me when I'm feelin' wild,
To be everlovin' and true and fair,
To run her fingers through my hair.

Refrain:
Come along and be my party doll.
Come along and be my party doll.
Come along and be my party doll.
I'll make love to you, to you,
I'll make love to you.

Well, I saw a gal walkin' down the street,
The kind of a gal I would love to meet.
She had blonde hair and eyes of blue.
Baby, I'm a-gonna have a party with you.

Refrain

Ev'ry man has gotta have a party doll,
To be with him when he's feelin' wild,
To be everlovin', true, and fair,
To run her fingers through his hair,
To run her fingers through his hair.

Refrain

Peggy Sue

Words and Music by Jerry Allison, Norman Petty and Buddy Holly

recorded by Buddy Holly

If you knew Peggy Sue,
Then you'd know why I feel blue
About Peggy,
'Bout my Peggy Sue
Oh, well, I love you, gal,
Yes, I love you, Peggy Sue.

Peggy Sue, Peggy Sue,
Oh, how my heart yearns for you,
Oh, Pa-heggy,
My Pa-heggy Sue.
Oh, well, I love you, gal,
Yes, I love you, Peggy Sue.

Peggy Sue, Peggy Sue,
Pretty, pretty, pretty, pretty Peggy Sue,
Oh, my Peggy
My Peggy Sue
Oh, well, I love you gal,
And I need you, Peggy Sue.

I love you, Peggy Sue,
With a love so rare and true,
Oh, Peggy,
My Peggy Sue
Oh, well, I love you, gal
Yes, I want you,
Peggy Sue.

Please Mr. Postman

Words and Music by Robert Bateman, Georgia Dobbins, William Garrett,
Freddie Gorman and Brian Holland

recorded by The Marvelettes, The Beatles

Oh yes, wait a minute, Mister Postman.
Wait, Mister Postman.

Refrain:
Mister Postman look and see,
Is there a letter in your bag for me?
I've been waiting a long, long time,
Since I heard from that girl (boy) of mine.

There must be some word today,
From my girlfriend (boyfriend) so far away.
Please, Mister Postman look and see,
If there's a letter, a letter for me?
I've been standing here waiting, Mister
    Postman,
So patiently, for just a card or just a letter,
Saying that she's (he's) returning home to
    me.

Refrain

So many days you've passed me by,
See the tears standing in my eyes,
You didn't stop to make me feel better
By leaving me a card or a letter,
Mister Postman,
Mister Postman, look and see,
Is there a letter in your bag for me?
I've been waiting for such a long time
Since I heard from that girlfriend
    (boyfriend) of mine.

You gotta wait a minute, wait a minute,
    oh yeah.
Wait a minute, wait a minute, oh yeah.
You gotta wait a minute, wait a minute,
    oh yeah.
Check it and see
One more time for me.

You gotta wait a minute, wait a minute,
    oh yeah.
Mister Postman, oh yeah.
Deliver the letter,
The sooner the better.

Repeat and Fade:
You gotta wait a minute, wait a minute,
    oh yeah.
Wait a minute, wait a minute, oh yeah.
You gotta wait a minute, wait a minute,
    oh yeah.

Raindrops

Words and Music by Dee Clark

recorded by Dee Clark

Raindrops, so many raindrops.
It feels like raindrops
Falling from my eye-eyes,
Falling from my eyes.

Since my love has left me, I'm so all alone,
I would bring her back to me
But I don't know where she's gone,
I don't know where she's gone.

There must be a cloud in my head.
Rain keeps falling from my eye-eyes.
Oh, no, it can't be teardrops,
'Cause a man ain't supposed to cry.

So it must be raindrops, so many raindrops.
It feels like raindrops
Falling from my eye-eyes,
Falling from my eyes.

Ready Teddy

Words and Music by John Marascalco and Robert Blackwell

recorded by Little Richard, Elvis Presley

Ready, set, go man go,
I got a girl that I love so.

Refrain:
I'm ready ready ready Teddy,
I'm ready ready ready Teddy,
I'm ready ready ready Teddy,
I'm ready ready ready to a-rock 'n' roll.

Going to the corner, pick up my sweetie pie.
She's my rock 'n' roll baby, she's the apple of my eye.

Refrain

Well, the flat top cats and the dungaree dolls
Are headed for the gym to the sock hop ball.
The joint is really jumpin', the cats are goin' wild.
The music really sends me. I dig that crazy style.

Refrain

Gonna kick off my shoes, roll up my faded jeans,
Grab my rock 'n' roll baby, pour on the steam.
I shuffle to the left. I shuffle to the right.
Gonna rock 'n' roll till the early, early night.

Refrain

Return to Sender

Words and Music by Otis Blackwell and Winfield Scott

recorded by Elvis Presley

I gave a letter to the postman; He put it in his sack.
Bright and early next morning he brought my letter back.

Refrain:
She wrote up on it:
Return to sender, address unknown.
No such number, no such zone.

We had a quarrel, a lover's spat.
I write to say I'm sorry but my letter keeps coming back.

So then I dropped it in the mailbox
And sent it Special D.
Bright and early next morning, it came right back to me.

Refrain

This time I'm gonna take it myself and put it right in her hand.
And if it comes back the very next day,
Then I'll understand the writing on it.

Twice:
Return to sender, address unknown.
No such number, no such zone.

Rock and Roll Is Here to Stay

Words and Music by David White

recorded by Danny & The Juniors

Rock, rock, rock,
Oh baby, rock, rock, rock,
Oh baby, rock, rock, rock,
Oh baby, rock, rock, rock,
Oh baby.

Rock and roll is here to stay,
And it will never die.
It was meant to be that way,
Though I don't know why.
I don't care what people say,
Rock and roll is here to stay!
We don't care what people say,
Rock and roll is here to stay.

Rock and roll will always be,
I dig it to the end.
It'll go down in history,
Just you watch, my friend.
Rock and roll will always be,
It'll go down in history.
Rock and roll will always be,
It'll go down in history.

Ev'rybody rock, ev'rybody rock,
Ev'rybody rock, ev'rybody rock.
Come on, ev'rybody rock and roll.
Ev'rybody rock and roll.
Ev'rybody rock and roll.
Ev'rybody rock and roll.
Ev'rybody rock and roll.
Come on, ev'rybody rock and roll.

If you don't like rock and roll,
Just think what you've been missin',
But if you like to bop and stroll,
Walk around and listen.
Let's all start to rock and roll,
Ev'rybody rock and roll.
We don't care what people say,
Rock and roll is here to stay.

Rock and roll will always be,
I dig it to the end.
It'll go down in history,
Just you watch, my friend.
Rock and roll will always be,
It'll go down in history.
Rock and roll will always be,
It'll go down in history.

Rock Around the Clock

Words and Music by Max C. Freedman and Jimmy DeKnight

recorded by Bill Haley & His Comets

One, two, three o'clock, four o'clock rock
Five, six, seven o'clock, eight o'clock rock
Nine, ten, eleven o'clock, twelve o'clock rock
We're gonna rock around the clock tonight

Put your glad rags on and join me, Hon
We'll have some fun when the clock strikes one.

Refrain:
We're gonna rock around the clock tonight
We're gonna rock, rock, rock, 'til broad daylight
We're gonna rock, gonna rock around the clock tonight

When the clock strikes two, and three and four
If the band slows down we'll yell for more

Refrain

When the chimes ring five and six and seven
We'll be rockin' up in seventh heav'n

Refrain

When it's eight, nine, ten, eleven, too
I'll be goin' strong and so will you

Refrain

When the clock strike twelve, we'll cool off, then
Start a rockin' 'round the clock again

Refrain

Romeo and Juliet (Just Like)

Words and Music by Freddie Gorman and Bob Hamilton

recorded by The Reflections

Finding a job tomorrow morning,
Got a little something I want to do.
Gonna buy something I can ride in,
Take my girl dating at the drive-in.
Our love's gonna be written down in history,
Just like Romeo and Juliet.

I'm gonna buy her pretty presents,
Just like the ones in the catalog.
Gonna show her how much I love her,
Let her know that one way or the other,
Our love's gonna be written down in history,
Just like Romeo and Juliet.

Talk about love and romance,
Just wait till I get myself straight.
I'm a gonna put Romeo's fame
Right smack dab outta date.

Right now I'm speculating,
Wonder what tomorrow's gonna really bring.
If I don't find work tomorrow,
It's gonna be heartaches and sorrow.
Our love's gonna be destroyed by a tragedy,
Just like Romeo and Juliet.

A Rose and a Baby Ruth

Words and Music by John D. Loudermilk

recorded by George Hamilton IV

We had a quarrel, a teenage quarrel.
Now I'm as blue as I know how to be.
I can't see you at your home.
I can't even call you on the phone.
So I'm sending you this present
Just to prove I was telling the truth.

Dear, I believe you won't laugh when you receive
This rose and a Baby Ruth.
I could have sent you an orchid of some kind,
But that's all I had in my jeans at the time.
So I'm sending you this present,
And just to prove I was telling the truth,
I'll kiss you too, then I'll hand to you
A rose and a Baby Ruth.

Rubber Ball

Words and Music by Aaron Schroeder and Ann Orlowski

recorded by Bobby Vee

I'm like a rubber ball, baby, that's all that I am to you.
(Bouncy, bouncy. Bouncy, bouncy.)
Just a rubber ball 'cause you think you can be true to two.
(Bouncy, bouncy. Bouncy, bouncy.)
You bounce my heart around, I don't even put you down,
And like a rubber ball I come bouncin' back to you.

If you stretch my love till it's thin enough to tear,
I'll just stretch my arms to reach you anywhere,
And like a rubber ball, I'll come bouncin' back to you.
Rubber ball, I'll come bouncin' back to you.
You bounce my heart around and I don't even put you down,
And like a rubber ball, I'll come bouncin' back to you.
Rubber ball, I'll come bouncin' back to you.

Bouncy, bouncy, bouncy, bouncy,
Bouncy, bouncy, bouncy, bouncy, e-e.

I'm like a rubber ball when on my shoulder you do tap.
(Bouncy, bouncy. Bouncy, bouncy.)
Just a rubber ball because my heart strings, they just snap.
(Bouncy, bouncy. Bouncy, bouncy.)
You go and squeeze me till I'm all aflame,
Then call me by some other guy's name.
But like a rubber ball, I come bouncin' back to you.
Rubber ball, I come bouncin' back to you.

Ruby Baby

Words and Music by Jerry Leiber and Mike Stoller

recorded by Dion

I love a girl and-a Ruby is her name.
This girl don't love me but I love her just the same.
Ruby, Ruby, how I want ya,
Like a ghost I'm a-gonna haunt ya.
Ruby, Ruby, Ruby, will you be mine?

Each time I see you, baby, my heart cries.
Tell ya, I'm gonna steal you away from all those guys.
From the happy day I met ya,
I made a bet that I was gonna get ya.
Ruby, Ruby, Ruby, will you be mine?

Four Times:
Ruby, Ruby, Ruby, baby.

I love this girl, I said-a Ruby is her name.
When this girl looks at me, she just sets my soul aflame.
Got some huggin' and kisses too, yeah,
And I'm gonna give them-a all to you.
Now listen, Ruby, Ruby, when will you be mine?
Ruby, Ruby, when will you be mine?

Run to Him

Words and Music by Gerry Goffin and Jack Keller

recorded by Bobby Vee

If you've found another guy {girl} who
Satisfies you more than I do
Run to him {her}, I'll step aside.

And if you think his {her} lips can kiss you
Better than my lips can kiss you,
Run to him {her}, forget my pride.

If someone else's arms can hold you
Better than my arms can hold you,
Go to him {her}, and show to him {her} all your devotion.

If somebody else can make you
Happier than I can make you
Run to him {her}, my eyes will dry.

But, if it's me you want to love you,
I'll be more than glad to love you,
Love you till your life is done
But darling if I'm not the one,
Then run to him {her}, my eyes will dry.

But, if it's me you want to love you,
I'll be more than glad to love you,
Love you till your life is done
But darling if I'm not the one,
Then run to him {her}, my eyes will dry.

Runaway

Words and Music by Del Shannon and Max Crook

recorded by Del Shannon

As I walk along I wonder
What went wrong with our love,
A love that was so strong.
And as I still walk on,
I think of the things we've done together,
While our hearts were young.

I'm a-walkin' in the rain.
Tears are fallin' and I feel a pain,
A-wishin' you were here by me
To end this misery.
And I wonder, wo-wo-wo-wo-wonder
Why, why-why-why-why-why she ran away,
And I wonder where she will stay,
My little runaway, run-run-run-run-runaway.

Sad Movies (Make Me Cry)

Words and Music by John D. Loudermilk

recorded by Sue Thompson

He said he had to work so I went to the show alone.
They turned down the lights and turned the projector on.
And just as the news of the world started to begin,
I saw my darling and my best friend walk in.

Though I was sitting there, they didn't see.
And so they sat right down in front of me.
And when he kissed her lips, I almost died.
And in the middle of the color cartoon, I started to cry.

Oh, sad movies always make me cry.
Oh, sad movies always make me cry.
So I got up and slowly walked on home.
And mama saw the tears and said, "What's wrong?"
And so to keep from telling her a lie,
I just said sad movies make me cry.

Save the Last Dance for Me

Words and Music by Doc Pomus and Mort Shuman

recorded by The Drifters

You can dance ev'ry dance
With the one that gives you the eye;
Let him hold you tight.
You can smile ev'ry smile
For the one that holds your hand
In the pale moonlight.

Refrain:
Just don't forget who's taking you home
And in whose arms you're gonna be.
So darlin', save the last dance for me.

Oh, I know that the music is fine,
Like sparkling wine;
Go and have your fun.
Laugh and sing, but while we're apart
Don't give your heart
To anyone.

Refrain

Baby, don't you know I love you so?
Can't you feel it when we touch?
I will never, never let you go.
I love you, oh, so much.

You can dance, go and carry on
Till the night is gone,
Till it's time to go.
If he asks if you're all alone,
Can he take you home,
You've got to tell him no.

'Cause don't forget who's taking you home,
And in whose arms you're gonna be.
So darlin', save the last dance for me.

Scotch and Soda

Words and Music by Dave Guard

recorded by The Kingston Trio

Scotch and soda, mud in your eye,
Baby, do I feel high, oh me, oh my,
Do I feel high.
Dry martini, jigger of gin,
Oh, what a spell you've got me in, oh, my,
Do I feel high.

People won't believe me,
They'll think that I'm jesting.
But I could feel the way I feel,
And still be on the wagon.
All I need is one of your smiles,
Sunshine of your eyes, or me, oh my,
Do I feel higher than a kite can fly!
Give me lovin', baby, I feel high.

Sea of Love

Words and Music by George Khoury and Philip Baptiste

recorded by Phil Phillips with The Twilights

Do you remember when we met,
That's the day I knew you were my pet.
I want to tell you
Just how much I love you.

Come with me my love
To the sea, the sea of love.
I want to tell you
Just how much I love you.

Come with me
To the sea
Of love.

Repeat Verse 1

Come with me
To the sea
Of love.

Come with me
My love
To the sea,
The sea of love.

I want to tell you
Just how much I love you.
I want to tell you,
Oh, how much
I love you.

Sealed with a Kiss

Words by Peter Udell
Music by Gary Geld

recorded by Brian Hyland

Though we gotta say good-bye for the summer,
Darling, I promise you this:
I'll send you all my love ev'ry day in a letter,
Sealed with a kiss.

Guess it's gonna be a cold, lonely summer,
But I'll fill the emptiness.
I'll send you all my love ev'ry day in a letter,
Sealed with a kiss.

I'll see you in the sunlight.
I'll hear your voice ev'rywhere.
I'll run to tenderly hold you,
But, darling, you won't be there.

I don't wanna say good-bye for the summer,
Knowing the love we'll miss.
Oh, let us make a pledge to meet in September,
And seal it with a kiss.

Sh-Boom (Life Could Be a Dream)

Words and Music by James Keyes, Claude Feaster, Carl Feaster, Floyd McRae and James Edwards

recorded by The Crew-Cuts, The Chords

Hey nonny ding dong, a-lang a-lang a-lang.
Boom ba-doh, ba-doo ba-doo.

Refrain:
Oh, life could be a dream,
(Sh-boom) If I could take you up in paradise up above.
(Sh-boom) If you would tell me I'm the only one that you love,
Life could be a dream, sweetheart.

(Hello, hello again, sh-boom, and hopin' we'll meet again.)

Oh, life could be a dream,
(Sh-boom) If only all my precious plans would come true.
(Sh-boom) If you would let me spend my whole life lovin' you,
Life could be a dream, sweetheart.

Ev'ry time I look at you,
Something is on my mind.
If you'd do what I want you to,
Baby, we'd be so fine.

Refrain

Twice:
Sh-boom sh-boom, ya-da-da da-da-da da-da-da-da.
Sh-boom sh-boom, ya-da-da da-da-da da-da-da-da.
Sh-boom sh-boom, ya-da-da da-da-da da-da-da-da, sh-boom.

Ev'ry time I look at you,
Something is on my mind.
If you'd do what I want you to,
Baby, we'd be so fine.

Refrain

Shake, Rattle and Roll

Words and Music by Charles Calhoun

Recorded by Bill Haley & His Comets

Get out from that kitchen
And rattle those pots and pans.
Get out from that kitchen
And rattle those pots and pans.
Well, roll my breakfast,
'Cause I'm a hungry man.

Refrain:
Shake, rattle, and roll.
Shake, rattle, and roll.
Shake, rattle, and roll.
Shake, rattle, and roll.
You never do nothin'
To save your doggone soul.

Wearin' those dresses,
Your hair done up so right.
Wearin' those dresses,
Your hair done up so right.
You look so warm,
But your heart is cold as ice.

Refrain

I'm like a one-eyed cat,
Peepin' in a seafood store.
I'm like a one-eyed cat,
Peepin' in a seafood store.
I can look at you,
Tell you don't love me no more.

I believe you're doin' me wrong,
And now I know.
I believe you're doin' me wrong,
And now I know.
The more I work,
The faster my money goes.

Refrain

Sherry

Words and Music by Bob Gaudio

recorded by The 4 Seasons

Sherry, Sherry baby,
Sherry, Sherry baby.

Sherry baby, Sherry baby,
Sherry, can you come out tonight?
Come, come, come out tonight.
Sherry baby, Sherry baby,
Sherry, can you come out tonight?

Why don't you come on to my twist party?
Come on where the bright moon shines.
Come on, we'll dance the night away.
I'm gonna make you mine.

Sherry baby, Sherry baby,
Sherry, can you come out tonight?
Come, come, come out tonight.
Come, come, come out tonight.

You better ask your mama, Sherry baby.
Tell her ev'rything is all right.
Why don't you come on, put your red dress on?
Come on, mm, you look so fine.
Come on, move it nice and easy.
Girl, you make me lose my mind.

Sherry baby, Sherry baby,
Sherry, can you come out tonight?
Come, come, come out tonight.
Come, come, come out tonight.
Sherry baby, Sherry baby,
Come, come, come out tonight.

The Shoop Shoop Song (It's in His Kiss)

Words and Music by Rudy Clark

Recorded by Betty Everett

Does he love me? I wanna know.
How can I tell if he loves me so?
(Is it in his eyes?) Oh, no, you'll be deceived.
(Is it in his eyes?) Oh, no, you'll make believe.
If you wanna know if he loves you so,
It's in his kiss.

(Is it in his face?) No, no, that's just his charm.
(In his warm embrace?) No, that's just his arm.
If you wanna know if he loves you so,
It's in his kiss.

Refrain:
Hug him and squeeze him tight,
And find out what you wanna know.
If it's love, if it really is,
It's there in his kiss.

(About the way he acts?) Oh, no, that's not the way,
And you're not list'nin' to all that I say.
If you wanna know if he loves you so,
It's in his kiss.

Refrain

It's in his kiss. (That's where it is.)
It's in his kiss. (That's where it is.)

Shop Around

Words and Music by Berry Gordy and William "Smokey" Robinson

recorded by The Miracles

When I became of age,
My mother called me to her side.
She said, "Son, you're growing up now.
Pretty soon you'll take a bride."
And then she said,

Just because you've become a young man
now,
There's still some things that you don't
understand now.
Before you ask some girl for her hand now,
Keep your freedom for as long as you can
now.

Refrain:
My mama told me, you better shop around.
Oh, yeah, you better shop around.

Ah, there's some things that I want you to
know now.
Just as sure as the winds gonna blow now,
The women come and the women gonna go
now.
Before you tell 'em that you love 'em so now,

Refrain

Try to get yourself a bargain, son.
Don't be sold on the very first one.
Pretty girls come a dime a dozen.
A-try to find one who's gonna give you true
lovin'.
Before you take a girl and say "I do," now,
Make sure she's in love with you now.
My mama told me, you better shop around.

Try to get yourself a bargain, son.
Don't be sold on the very first one.
Pretty girls come a dime a dozen.
A-try to find one who's gonna give you true
lovin'.
Before you take a girl and say "I do," now,
Make sure she's in love with you now.
Make sure that her love is true now.
I hate to see you feelin' sad and blue now.
My mama told me, you better shop around.

Short Shorts

Words and Music by Bill Crandall, Tom Austin, Bob Gaudio and Bill Dalton

recorded by The Royal Teens

Boys:
Who wears short shorts?

Girls:
We wear short shorts.

Boys:
Bless 'em, short shorts.

Girls:
We like short shorts.

Boys:
Who wears short shorts?

Girls:
We wear short shorts.

Sidewalk Surfin'

Words and Music by Roger Christian and Brian Wilson

recorded by Jan & Dean

Grab your board and go sidewalk surfin' with me.

Don't be afraid to try the newest sport around.
(Bust your buns, bust your buns now.)
It's catchin' on in every city and town.
You can do the tricks the surfers do,
Just try the Quasimodo or the Coffin too.
Why don't you grab your board and go sidewalk surfin' with me.

You'll prob'ly wipe out when first try to shoot the curve.
(Bust your buns, bust your buns now.)
Takin' gas in a bush takes a lot of nerve.
Those hopscotch poledads and pedestrians, too, will bug ya.
Shout, "Cuyabunga," now and skate right on through.
Why don't you grab your board and go sidewalk surfin' with me.

You can do the tricks the surfers do,
Just try the Quasimodo or the Coffin too.
Why don't you grab your board and go sidewalk surfin' with me.

So get your girl and take her tandem down the street.
(Bust your buns, bust your buns now.)
Then she'll know you're an asphalt athlete.
The downhill grade, man, 'll give you a kick.
But if the sidewalk's cracked, you better pull out quick.
Why don't you grab your board and go sidewalk surfin' with me.
Skateboard with me, why don't you skateboard with me.
Grab your board and go sidewalk surfin' with me.
Skateboard with me, why don't you skateboard with me.

Shout

Words and Music by O'Kelly Isley, Ronald Isley and Rudolph Isley

recorded by The Isley Brothers

Refrain:
You know you make me wanna
(Shout!) Kick my heels up and
(Shout!) Throw my hands up and
(Shout!) Throw my head back and
(Shout!) Come on, now.

Don't forget to say you will.
Don't forget to say yeah, yeah, yeah.
(Say you will.) Say it right now, baby.
(Say you will.) Well, come on, come on.
(Say you will.) Say that you.
(Say you will.)

(Say!) Say that you love me.
(Say!) Say that you need me.
Say that you want me.
Say you wanna please me.
(Say!) Come on now.
(Say!) Come on now.
(Say!) Come on now.
(Say!) I still remember
When I used to be nine years old, hey yeah.
And I was a fool for you
From the bottom of my soul.
Yeah, yeah, now that I found you,
I will never let you go, no, no.
And if you ever leave me.
You know it's gonna hurt me so.

I want you to know,
I said, I want you to know right now.
You been good to me, sisters,
Much better than I been to myself,
So good, so good.
And if you ever leave me,
I don't want nobody else, hey, hey.
I said, I want you to know, yeah,
I said, I want you to know right now.

Refrain

(Shout!) Come on now.
(Shout!) Come on now.
(Shout!) Come on now.
(Shout!) Play it, Sister Allen, hey.

Hey (hey), hey (hey),
Hey, yea, yea, yea. (Hey, yea, yea, yea.)
Hey, yea, yea, yea. (Hey, yea, yea.)

Repeat Ad Lib:
(Shout!) A little bit softer now.

Four Times:
(Shout!) A little bit louder now.

(Shout!) Get on up.
(Shout!) Get on up.
(Shout!)

All right now, come on, basses.

Bum, bum, bum, bum,
Bum, bum, bum, bum, bum.
Bum, bum, bum, bum,
Bum, bum, bum, bum, bum, bum.
Come on now.
Come on now.

Twice:
Shoo-be do-wop do wop, wop, wop, wop.
Shoo-be-do-be do-wop, do wop, wop, wop.

Shout, shout, shout, whoa.
Shout, shout, shout, whoa.
Hey (hey), hey (hey).

Refrain

Don't forget to say yeah,
Yeah, yeah, yeah, yeah.
Say you will.
Say you will.

Spoken:
Now wait a minute.
All right, who was that?
You know you make me wanna shout.

Silhouettes

Words and Music by Frank C. Slay Jr. and Bob Crewe

recorded by The Rays, The Diamonds, Herman's Hermits

Took a walk and passed your house late last night,
All the shades were pulled and drawn 'way down tight;
From within a dim light cast
Two silhouettes on the shade,
Oh, what a lovely couple they made.

Put his arms around your waist, held you tight,
Kisses I could almost taste in the night,
Wondered why I'm not the guy
Who's silhouette's on the shade
I couldn't hide the tears in my eyes.

Lost control, and rang your bell, I was sore,
"Let me in or else I'll beat down your door."
When two strangers, who had been
Two silhouettes on the shade
Said to my shock, "You're on the wrong block."

Rushed down to your house with wings on my feet,
Loved you like I've never loved you my sweet,
Vowed that you and I would be
Two silhouettes on the shade
All of our days,
Two silhouettes on the shade.

Since I Don't Have You

Words and Music by James Beaumont, Janet Vogel, Joseph Verscharen, Walter Lester,
Lennie Martin, Joseph Rock and John Taylor

recorded by The Skyliners

I don't have plans and schemes
And I don't have daydreams.
I don't have anything
Since I don't have you.

I don't have fond desires
And I don't have happy hours.
I don't have anything
Since I don't have you.

I don't have happiness
And I guess I never will ever again.
When you walked out on me
In walked misery,
And he's been here since then.

Now I don't have much to share,
And I don't have one to care.
I don't have anything
Since I don't have you you you you
You you you you
You you you you
You.

Sincerely

Words and Music by Alan Freed and Harvey Fuqua

recorded by The McGuire Sisters

Sincerely, oh, yes, sincerely,
'Cause I love you so dearly.
Please say you'll be mine.
Sincerely, oh, you know how I love you.
I'll do anything for you;
Please say you'll be mine.

Oh, Lord, won't you tell me why I love that fella [girl] so?
He [she] doesn't want me.
Oh, I'll never, never, never, never let him [her] go.
Sincerely, oh, you know how I love you!
I'll do anything for you.
Please say you'll be mine.

Singing the Blues

Words and Music by Melvin Endsley

recorded by Guy Mitchell, Marty Robbins

Well, I never felt more like singing the blues
'Cause I never thought that I'd ever lose your love, dear.
Why'd you do me this way?

Well, I never felt more like crying all night
'Cause ev'rything's wrong and nothing ain't right without you.
You got me singing the blues.

The moon and stars no longer shine,
The dream is gone I thought was mine.
There's nothing left for me to do but cry over you.

Well, I never felt more like running away
But why should I go 'cause I couldn't stay without you.
You got me singing the blues.

(Seven Little Girls) Sitting in the Back Seat

Words by Bob Hilliard
Music by Lee Pockriss

recorded by Paul Evans

Seven little girls sitting in the back seat,
Huggin' and a-kissin' with Fred.
I said, "Why don't one of you come up and sit beside me?"
And this is what the seven girls said:

Refrain:
All together now, one, two, three!
Keep your mind on your driving,
Keep your hands on the wheel.
Keep your snoopy eyes on the road ahead.
We're havin' fun sittin' in the back seat
Kissin' and a-huggin' with Fred.

Drove through the town, drove through the country,
Showed them how a motor could go.
I said, "How do you like my triple carburetor?"
And one of 'em whispered low:

Refrain

Seven little girls smoochin' in the back seat,
Ev'ry one in love with Fred.
I said, "You don't need me, I'll get off at my house."
And this is what the seven girls said:

Refrain

Sixteen Candles

Words and Music by Luther Dixon and Allyson R. Khent

recorded by The Crests

Sixteen candles make a lovely light,
But not as bright as your eyes tonight.
Blow out the candles, make your wish come true,
For I'll be wishing that you love me too.

You're only sixteen, but you're my teenage queen.
You're the prettiest, loveliest girl I've ever seen.
Sixteen candles in my heart will glow
For ever and ever, for I love you so.

Sixteen Reasons (Why I Love You)

Words and Music by Bill Post and Doree Post

recorded by Connie Stevens

One—the way you hold my hand,
Two—your laughing eyes,
Three—the way you understand,
Four—your secret sighs.
They're all part of sixteen reasons
Why I love you.

Five—the way you comb your hair,
Six—your freckled nose,
Seven—the way you say you care,
Eight—your crazy clothes.
That's just half of sixteen reasons
Why I love you.

Nine—snuggling in the car,
Ten—your wish upon a star,
Eleven—whisp'ring on the phone,
Twelve—your kiss when we're alone,
Thirteen—the way you thrill my heart,
Fourteen—your voice so neat,
Fifteen—you say we'll never part,
Sixteen—our love's complete.
Those are all of sixteen reasons
Why I love you.

Soldier Boy

Words and Music by Luther Dixon and Florence Green

recorded by The Shirelles

Refrain:
Soldier boy,
Oh, my little soldier boy,
I'll be true to you.

You were my first love
And you'll be my last love.
I will never make you blue.
I'll be true to you.
In this whole world
You can love but one girl.
Let me be that one girl,
For I'll be true to you.

Wherever you go,
My heart will follow.
I love you so.
I'll be true to you.
Take my love with you
To any port or foreign shore.
Darling, you must feel for sure,
I'll be true to you.

Refrain

Speedoo

Words and Music by Esther Navarro

recorded by The Cadillacs

Bom, bom, bom,
Bom, bom, bom,
Bom, bom, bom, bom.

Now they up and call me Speedoo,
But my real name is Mister Earl.
Now they up and call me Speedoo,
But my real name is Mister Earl.
All for meetin' brand-new fellows
And for takin' other folks' girls.

Now they up and call me Speedoo,
'Cause I don't believe in wastin' time.
Now they up and call me Speedoo,
'Cause I don't believe in wastin' time.
Now I've known some pretty women
And I thought that would change their minds.

Well, now, some they call me Joe.
Some they call me Moe.
Best man is Speedoo;
He don't never take it slow.

Now they up and call me Speedoo,
But my real name is Mister Earl.
Now they up and call me Speedoo,
But my real name is Mister Earl.
Now they're gonna call me Speedoo,
Till they call off makin' pretty girls.

Bom, bom, bom,
Bom, bom, bom,
Bom, bom, bom, bom.

Splish Splash

Words and Music by Bobby Darin and Murray Kaufman

recorded by Bobby Darin

Splish Splash, I was taking a bath
Long about a Saturday night.
Rub-a-dub, just relaxing in the tub
Thinking everything was alright.
Well, I stepped out the tub, put my feet on
   the floor,
I wrapped the towel around me
And I opened the door, and then
Splish, Splash! I jumped back in the bath.
Well, how was I to know there was a party
   going on?

They was a-splishin' and a-splashin',
Reelin' with the feelin',
movin' and a-groovin',
Rockin' and a-rollin', yeah!

Bing bang, I saw the whole gang
Dancing on my living room rug, yeah!
Flip flop, they was doing the bop.
All the teens had the dancing bug.
There was lollipop with-a Peggy Sue
Good Golly, Miss Molly was-a even there, too!
Ah, well-a, splish splash, I forgot about the
   bath.
I went and put my dancing shoes on, yeah.

I was a-rollin' and a-strollin',
Reeling with the feelin',
Moving and a-groovin',
Splishin' and a-splashin', yeah!

Yes, I was a-splishin' and a-splashin',
I was a-rollin' and a-strollin',
Yeah, I was a-movin' and a-groovin',
We was a-reeling with the feeling,
We was a-rollin' and a-strollin',
Movin' with the groovin',
Splish splash, yeah!

Splishin' and a-splashin',
I was a-splishin' and a-splashin',
I was a-movin' and a-groovin',
Yeah, I was a-splishin' and a-splashin'.

Stand by Me

Words and Music by Ben E. King, Jerry Leiber and Mike Stoller

recorded by Ben E. King

When the night has come and the land is dark
And the moon is the only light we'll see.
No I won't be afraid, no I won't be afraid
Just as long as you stand,
Stand by me.

Refrain:
So darling, darling,
Stand by me,
Oh, stand by me,
Oh, stand,
Stand by me,
Stand by me.

If the sea that we look upon should tumble and fall
Or the mountain crumble in the sea.
I won't cry, no I won't shed a tear
Just as long as you stand,
Stand by me.

Refrain

Whenever you're in trouble won't you stand by me
Oh, stand by me,
Oh, stand by me,
Stand by me.

Refrain

Stay

Words and Music by Maurice Williams

recorded by Maurice Williams & The Zodiacs

Dance just a little bit longer.
Please, please, please, please
Tell me that you're goin' to.
Now, your daddy don't mind
And your mommy don't mind.
Could we have another dance, dear,
Just-a one more, one more time?

Oh, won't you stay
Just a little bit longer?
Please let me dance.
Please say that you will.

Stuck on You

Words and Music by Aaron Schroeder and J. Leslie McFarland

recorded by Elvis Presley

You can shake an apple off an apple tree.
Shake-a, shake-a, sugar, but you'll never shake me, uh-uh-uh.
No siree, uh-uh.
I'm gonna stick like glue,
Stick because I'm stuck on you.

Gonna run my fingers through your long black hair.
Squeeze you tighter than a grizzly bear, uh-huh-huh.
Yes siree, uh-huh.
I'm gonna stick like glue,
Stick because I'm stuck on you.

Hide in the kitchen, hide in the hall,
Ain't gonna do you no good at all.
'Cause once I catch ya and the kissin' starts,
A team o' wild horses couldn't tear us apart.

Try to take a tiger from his daddy's side.
That's how love is gonna keep us tied, uh-huh-huh.
Yes siree, uh-huh.
I'm gonna stick like glue,
Yay, yay, because I'm stuck on you.

Stupid Cupid

Words and Music by Howard Greenfield and Neil Sedaka

recorded by Connie Francis

Stupid Cupid, you're a real mean guy.
I'd like to clip your wings so you can't fly.
I am in love and it's a cryin' shame,
And I know that you're the one to blame.
Hey, hey, set me free.
Stupid Cupid, stop pickin' on me.

I can't do my homework and I can't think straight.
I meet him ev'ry mornin' 'bout a half past eight.
I'm actin' like a lovesick fool.
You even got me carryin' his books to school.
Hey, hey, set me free.
Stupid Cupid, stop pickin' on me.

You mixed me up but good right from the very start.
Hey, go play Robin Hood with somebody else's heart.

You got me jumpin' like a crazy clown,
And I don't feature what you're puttin' down.
Since I kissed his lovin' lips of wine,
The thing that bothers me is that I like it fine.
Hey, hey, set me free.
Stupid Cupid, stop pickin' on me.

Sugartime

Words and Music by Charles Phillips and Odis Echols

recorded by The McGuire Sisters

Sugar in the mornin',
Sugar in the evenin',
Sugar at suppertime.
Be my little sugar
And love me all the time.

Honey in the mornin',
Honey in the evenin',
Honey at suppertime.
You'll be my little honey
And love me all the time.

Put your arms around me
And swear by the stars above,
You'll be mine forever
In a heaven of love.

Repeat Verse 1

Now sugar time is anytime
That you're near or just appear.
So don't you roam,
Just be my honeycomb.
We'll live in a heaven of love.

Repeat All Except Last Verse

Surf City

Words and Music by Brian Wilson and Jan Berry

recorded by Jan & Dean

Two girls for ev'ry boy!

I bought a thirty-four Ford wagon and we call it a woody.
Surf City, here we come!
You know it's not very cherry as an oldie but a goodie.
Surf City, here we come!
Well, it ain't got a back seat or a rear window,
But it still gets me where I wanna go.

Refrain:
And I'm goin' to Surf City 'cause it's two to one.
You know I'm goin' to Surf City, gonna have some fun.
Yeah, I'm goin' to Surf City 'cause it's two to one.
You know I'm goin' to Surf City, gonna have some fun.
Two girls for ev'ry boy!

They say they never roll the streets up 'cause there's always somethin' going.
Surf City, here we come!
They're either out surfin' or they got a party goin'.
Surf City, here we come!
There's two swingin' honeys for ev'ry guy,
And all you gotta do is just wink your eye.

Refrain

And if my woody breaks down on me somewhere on my surf route,
Surf City, here we come.
I'll strap my board to my back and hitch a ride in my wetsuit.
Surf City, here we come!
When I get to Surf City I'll be shootin' the curl
And pickin' out the parties for the surfer girl.

Surfin' U.S.A.

Words by Brian Wilson
Music by Chuck Berry

recorded by The Beach Boys

If everybody had an ocean across the U.S.A.
Then everybody'd be surfin', like California.
You'd see them wearin' their baggies
Huarachi sandals too.
A bushy, bushy blond hairdo,
Surfin' U.S.A.

You'll catch 'em surfin' at Del Mar, Ventura County Line,
Santa Cruz and Tressels, Australia's Narabine,
All over Manhattan and down Doheny way.
Everybody's gone surfin', surfin' U.S.A.

Will all be plannin' out a route
We're gonna take real soon,
We're waxing down our surf boards,
We can't wait for June.
We'll all be gone for the summer,
We're on safari to stay.
Tell the teacher we're surfin',
Surfin' U.S.A.

At Haggarty's and Swami's, Pacific Palisades,
San Onofre and Sunset Redondo Beach, L.A.
All over La Jolla, and at Waiamea Bay.
Everybody's gone surfin',
Surfin' U.S.A.

Surrender

Original Italian Lyrics by G.B. De Curtis
English Words and Adaptation by Doc Pomus and Mort Shuman
Music by E. De Curtis

recorded by Elvis Presley

When we kiss my heart's on fire,
Burning with a strange desire.
And I know each time I kiss you
That your heart's on fire too.

So, my darling, please surrender
All your love so warm and tender.
Let me hold you in my arms, dear,
While the moon shines bright above.

All the stars will tell the story
Of our love and all its glory
Let us take this night of magic
And make it a night of love.

Won't you please surrender to me,
Your lips, your arms, your heart, dear.
Be mine forever;
Be mine tonight.

Suspicion

Words and Music by Doc Pomus and Mort Shuman

Recorded by Terry Stafford

Ev'ry time you kiss me,
I'm still not certain that you love me.
Ev'ry time you hold me,
I'm still not certain that you care.
Though you keep on saying
You really, really, really love me,
Do you speak the same words
To someone else when I'm not there?

Refrain:
Suspicion torments my heart.
Suspicion keeps us apart.
Suspicion, why torture me!

Ev'rytime you call me
And tell me we should meet tomorrow,
I can't help but think that
You're meeting someone else tonight.
Why should our romance just
A-keep on causing me such sorrow?
Why am I so doubtful
Whenever you're out of sight?

Refrain

Darling, if you love me,
I beg you, wait a little longer.
Wait until I drive all
These foolish fears out of my mind.
How I hope and pray that
Our love will keep on growing stronger.
Maybe I'm suspicious
'Cause true love is so hard to find.

Refrain

Take Good Care of My Baby

Words and Music by Gerry Goffin and Carole King

recorded by Bobby Vee

My tears are fallin'
'Cause you're takin' her away,
And though it really hurts me so,
There's somethin' that I gotta say.

Take good care of my baby,
Please don't ever make her blue.
Just tell her that you love her,
Make sure you're thinkin' of her
In ev'ything you say and do.
Take good care of my baby,
Don't you ever make her cry.
Just let your love surround her,
Paint a rainbow all around her.
Don't let her see a cloudy sky.

Once upon a time that little girl was mine.
If I'd been true, I know she'd never be with you.
So take good care of my baby,
Be just as kind as you can be.
And if you should discover
That you don't really love her,
Just send my baby back home to me.

Tears on My Pillow

Words and Music by Sylvester Bradford and Al Lewis

recorded by Little Anthony & The Imperials

You don't remember me,
But I remember you.
'Twas not so long ago
You broke my heart in two.
Tears on my pillow, pain in my heart,
Caused by you.

If we could start anew,
I wouldn't hesitate.
I'd gladly take you back
And tempt the hand of fate.
Tears on my pillow, pain in my heart,
Caused by you.

Love is not a gadget, love is not a toy.
When you find the one you love
She'll fill your heart with joy.

Before you go away,
My darling, think of me.
There may be still a chance
To end my misery.
Tears on my pillow, pain in my heart,
Caused by you.

(Let Me Be Your) Teddy Bear

Words and Music by Kal Mann and Bernie Lowe

recorded by Elvis Presley

Baby, let me be your lovin' teddy bear.
Put a chain around my neck
And lead me anywhere.
Oh, let me be your teddy bear.

I don't want to be your tiger
'Cause tigers play too rough.
I don't want to be your lion
'Cause lions ain't the kind you love enough.

Refrain:
Just wanna be your teddy bear.
Put a chain around my neck
And lead me anywhere.
Oh, let me be your teddy bear.

Baby, let me be around you ev'ry night.
Run your fingers through my hair
And cuddle me real tight.
Oh, let me be your teddy bear.

I don't want to be your tiger
'Cause tigers play too rough.
I don't want to be your lion
'Cause lions ain't the kind you love enough.

Refrain

Teen Angel

Words and Music by Jean Surrey

recorded by Mark Dinning

That fateful night the car was stalled
Upon the railroad track.
I pulled you out and we were safe,
But you went running back.

Refrain:
Teen angel, can you hear me?
Teen angel, can you see me?
Are you somewhere up above,
And am I still your own true love?

What was it you were looking for
That took your life that night?
They said they found my high school ring
Clutched in your fingers tight.

Refrain

Just sweet sixteen, and now you're gone;
They've taken you away.
I'll never kiss your lips again;
They buried you today.

Refrain

Teen angel, teen angel, answer me, please.

A Teenager in Love

Words and Music by Doc Pomus and Mort Shuman

recorded by Dion & The Belmonts

Each time we have a quarrel, it almost breaks my heart,
'Cause I'm so afraid that we will have to part.
Each night I ask the stars up above,
Why must I be a teenager in love?

One day I feel so happy, next day I feel so sad.
I guess I'll learn to take the good with the bad.
Each night I ask the stars up above,
Why must I be a teenager in love?

I cried a tear for nobody but you.
I'll be a lonely one if you should say we're through.

If you want to make me cry, that won't be so hard to do.
And if you should say good-bye, I'll still go on loving you.
Each night I ask the stars up above,
Why must I be a teenager in love?

Tell Her (Tell Him)

Words and Music by Bert Russell

recorded by The Exciters

I know somethin' about love;
You gotta want it bad.
If that guy's got into your blood,
Go out and get him.
If you want him to be
The very part of you
Makes you want to breathe,
Here's the thing to do.

Refrain:
Tell him that you're never gonna leave him.
Tell him that you're always gonna love him.
Tell him, tell him, tell him,
   tell him right now.

I know something about love;
You gotta show it and
Make him see the moon up above.
Reach out and get it.
If you want him,
Makes your heart sing out,
If you want him to
Only think of you.

Refrain

Ever since the world began,
It's been that way for man.
And women were created
To make love their destiny.
Then why should true love be so
   complicated?
Oh yeah, uh-huh.

I know somethin' about love;
Gotta take it and show him
What the world's made of.
One kiss will prove it.
If you want him to be
Always by your side,
Take his hand tonight,
Swallow your foolish pride.

Refrain

That'll Be the Day

Words and Music by Jerry Allison, Norman Petty and Buddy Holly

recorded by The Crickets

Well, you give me all your lovin'
And your turtle-dovin',
All your hugs an' your money too;
Well, you know you love me, baby,
Until you tell me, maybe, that someday, well,
I'll be through! Well,

Refrain:
That'll be the day,
When you say goodbye,
Yes, that'll be the day,
When you make me cry,
Ah you say you're gonna leave,
You know it's a lie,
'Cause that'll be the day when I die.

Well, when Cupid shot his dart,
He shot it at your heart,
So if we ever part and I leave you,
You say you told me an' you
Told me boldly, that some way, well,
I'll be through. Well,

Refrain

That's Why (I Love You So)

Words and Music by Berry Gordy, Gwen Gordy Fuqua and Tyran Carlo

recorded by Jackie Wilson

The way you make me feel like I belong;
The way you make me right when I am wrong;
The way you sacrifice just for me;
Just how lucky can a poor man be?

Refrain:
That is why.
(That's why I love you so.)
That is why.
(That's why I love you so.)
Don't you know, baby?
(That's why I love you so.)
Yeah, yeah, yeah, I want the world to know.

The way you rub my back when I'm in pain;
The way you soothe me so I won't complain;
And then you kiss me with your ruby red lips;
It thrills me so, I turn a back-over flip.

Refrain

If Shakespeare thought that Juliet
Really loved Romeo from the time they met,
Uh he would blow his top if he could see
Just how you've been loving me.

Repeat Verse 2

Refrain

There Goes My Baby

Words and Music by Jerry Leiber, Mike Stoller, Ben E. Nelson, Lover Patterson and George Treadwell

recorded by The Drifters

There goes my baby,
Movin' on down the line.
Wonderin' where, wonderin' where,
Wonderin' where she is bound.
I broke her heart and made her cry.
Now I'm alone, so all alone.
What can I do, what can I do?

(There goes my baby.
There goes my baby.
There she goes.)

Yes, I wanna know.
Did she love me?
Did she really love me?
Was she just playing me for a fool?
I wonder why she left me.
Why did she leave me
So all alone, so all alone?

I was gonna tell her that I love her
And that I need her
Beside my side to be my guide.
I wanna know where is my,
Where is my baby?
I want my baby.
I need my baby, yes.
Oh, oh, oh.

Things

Words and Music by Bobby Darin

recorded by Bobby Darin

Ev'ry night I sit here by my window (window),
Staring at the lonely avenue (avenue),
Watching lovers holding hands and laughing (laughing),
And thinkin' 'bout the things we used to do.

Refrain:
(Thinkin' of things) Like a walk in the park,
(Things) Like a kiss in the dark,
(Things) Like a sailboat ride,
(Yeah, yeah) What about the night we cried?
Things like a lover's vow,
Things that we don't do now,
Thinkin' 'bout the things we used to do.

Memories are all I have to cling to (cling to),
And heartaches are the friends I'm talking to (talking to).
When I'm not thinkin' of a-just how much I love you (love you),
Well, I'm thinkin' 'bout the things we used to do.

Refrain

I still can hear the jukebox softly playing (playing),
And the face I see each day belongs to you (belongs to you).
Though there's not a single sound and there's nobody else around,
Well, there's a-just me thinkin' 'bout the things we used to do.

Refrain

And the heartaches are the friends I'm talking to.
You got me thinkin' 'bout the things we used to do.
Starin' at the lonely avenue.

This I Swear

Words and Music by Joseph Rock, James Beaumont, Janet Vogel, Joseph Verscharen, Walter Lester, John Taylor and Lennie Martin

recorded by The Skyliners

If you can't depend on no one else,
And you're try'n' to make it through life all by yourself,
Look to me. I'll be there.
I'll come to your aid no matter where.

Refrain:
I'll treat you good. I'll be fair,
Give you good lovin' always, this I swear.
Feel so good about it, ooh, ooh, baby.
Ooh, ooh.

If life's ups and downs are too much for you to stand,
And you searched so long in vain for that helpin' hand,
Look to me. I'm the one.
'Cause life without love sure ain't no fun.

Refrain

Too Much

Words and Music by Lee Rosenberg and Bernie Weinman

recorded by Elvis Presley

Honey, I love you too much.
Need your lovin' too much.
Want the thrill of your touch.
Gee, I can't hold you too much.
You do all the livin' while I do all the givin'
'Cause I love you too much.

You spend all my money too much.
Have to share you, honey, too much.
When I want some lovin', you're gone.
Don't you know you're treatin' me wrong.
Now you got me started, don't you leave me brokenhearted,
'Cause I love you too much.

Refrain:
Need your lovin' all the time,
Need your huggin'; please be mine.
Need you near me; stay real close.
Please, please hear me, you're the most.
Now you got me started, don't you leave me brokenhearted,
'Cause I love you too much.

Ev'ry time I kiss your sweet lips,
I can feel my heart go flip flip.
I'm such a fool for your charms,
Take me back, my baby, in your arms.
Like to hear you sighin' even though I know you're lyin',
'Cause I love you too much.

Refrain

Travelin' Man

Words and Music by Jerry Fuller

recorded by Ricky Nelson

I'm a travelin' man,
And I've made a lot o' stops all over the world.
And in every port I own the heart
Of at least one lovely girl.

I've a pretty señorita waiting for me
Down in old Mexico.
If you're ever in Alaska, stop and see
My cute little Eskimo.

Oh my sweet fraulein down in Berlin town
Makes my heart start to yearn.
And my China doll down in old Hong Kong
Waits for my return.

Pretty Polynesian baby over the sea,
I remember the night
When we walked in the sands of Waikiki
And I held you, oh, so tight.

Repeat All

Oh, I'm a travelin' man.
Yes, I'm a travelin' man.

Turn Me Loose

Words and Music by Doc Pomus and Mort Shuman

recorded by Fabian

Turn me loose, turn me loose, I say.
This is the first time I ever felt this way.
Gonna get a thousand kicks, gonna kiss a thousand chicks,
So turn me loose.

Turn me loose, turn me loose, I say.
Gonna rock and roll long as the band's gonna play.
Gonna holler, gonna shout, gonna knock myself right out,
So turn me loose.

I've got some change in my pocket and I'm rarin' to go.
I'm takin' some chick to the picture show.
When I see her home and we kiss goodnight,
Turn me loose, turn me loose, turn me loose, turn me loose.

Turn me loose, turn me loose, I say.
Yes, today is gonna be the day.
I want you all to understand that now I am a man,
So turn me loose.

Tutti Frutti

Words and Music by Little Richard Penniman and Dorothy La Bostrie

recorded by Pat Boone, Little Richard

A bop bop a loom op
A lop bop boom!

Refrain:
Tutti frutti, au rutti,
Tutti frutti, au rutti,
Tutti frutti, au rutti,
Tutti frutti, au rutti,
A bop bop a loom op
A lop bop boom!

I got a gal, her name's Sue,
She knows just what to do.
I got a gal, her name's Sue,
She knows just what to do.
I've been to the east, I've been to the west,
But she's the gal I love the best.

Refrain

I got a gal, her name's Daisy,
She almost drives me crazy.
I got a gal, her name's Daisy,
She almost drives me crazy.
She's a real gone cookie, yes siree,
But pretty little Suzy's the gal for me.

Refrain

26 Miles (Santa Catalina)

Words and Music by Glen Larson and Bruce Belland

recorded by The Four Preps

Twenty-six miles across the sea,
Santa Catalina is a-waitin' for me.
Santa Catalina, the island of romance,
Romance, romance, romance.
Water all around it ev'rywhere,
Tropical trees and the salty air;
But for me the thing that's a-waitin' there's romance.

It seems so distant, twenty-six miles away,
Restin' in the water serene.
I'd work for anyone, even the Navy,
Who would float me to my island dream.
Twenty-six miles, so near yet far.
I'd swim with just some water wings and my guitar.
I can leave the wings but I'll need the guitar for romance,
Romance, romance, romance.

Twenty-six miles across the sea,
Santa Catalina is a-waitin' for me.
Santa Catalina, the island of romance.

A tropical heaven out in the ocean
Covered with trees and girls.
If I have to swim, I'd do it forever
Till I'm gazin' on those island pearls.
Forty kilometers in a leaky old boat,
Any old thing that'll stay afloat.
When we arrive we'll all promote romance,
Romance, romance, romance.

The Twist

Words and Music by Hank Ballard

recorded by Chubby Checker

Come on, baby, let's do the twist.
Come on, baby, let's do the twist.
Take me by my little hand and go like this:

Refrain:
Ee oh twist, baby, baby, twist.
('Round and around and around and a.)
Just, just like this.
('Round and around.)
Come on, little miss, and do the twist.
('Round and around.)

While Daddy is sleepin' and Mama ain't around,
While Daddy is sleepin' and Mama ain't around,
We're gonna twisty, twisty, twisty
Until we tear the house down.

Refrain

You should see my little sis.
You should see my little sis.
She knows how to rock,
And she knows how to twist.

Refrain

Twist and Shout

Words and Music by Bert Russell and Phil Medley

recorded by The Beatles, The Isley Brothers

Refrain:
Well, shake it up, baby, now (shake it up, baby).
Twist and shout (twist and shout).
Come on, come on, come on, come on, baby, now (come on baby).
Come on and work it on out (work it on out).

Well, work it on out (work it on out).
You know you look so good (look so good).
You know you got me goin' now (got me goin'),
Just like I knew you would (like I knew you would).

Refrain

You know you twist, little girl (twist, little girl).
You know you twist so fine (twist so fine).
Come on and twist a little closer now (twist a little closer)
And let me know that you're mine (let me know you're mine).

Ah, ah, ah, ah, ah.

Refrain

You know you twist, little girl (twist, little girl).
You know you twist so fine (twist so fine).
Come on and twist a little closer now (twist a little closer)
And let me know that you're mine (let me know you're mine).

Well, shake it, shake it, shake it, baby, now (shake it up baby).
Well, shake it, shake it, shake it, baby, now (shake it up baby).
Well, shake it, shake it, shake it, baby, now (shake it up baby).

Ah, ah, ah.

Under the Boardwalk

Words and Music by Artie Resnick and Kenny Young

recorded by The Drifters

Oh, when the sun beats down
And burns the tar up on the roof,
And your shoes get so hot
Your wish your tired feet were fireproof;
Under the boardwalk,
Down by the sea, yeah,
On a blanket with my baby's where I'll be.

Refrain:
(Under the boardwalk.)
Out of the sun,
(Under the boardwalk.)
We'll be havin' some fun.
(Under the boardwalk.)
People walkin' above
(Under the boardwalk.)
We'll be fallin' in love
Under the boardwalk, boardwalk.

From the park you hear
The happy sound of a carousel.
You can almost taste the hot dogs
And French fries they sell.
Under the boardwalk,
Down by the sea, yeah,
On a blanket with my baby's where I'll be.

Refrain

Under the boardwalk,
Down by the sea, yeah,
On a blanket with my baby's where I'll be.

Refrain

Up on the Roof

Words and Music by Gerry Goffin and Carole King

recorded by The Drifters

When this old world starts getting' me down
And people are just too much for me to face,
I climb way up to the top of the stairs
And all my cares just drift right into space.

On the roof, it's peaceful as can be,
And there the world below don't bother me.

Let me tell you now,
When I come home feeling tired and beat,
I'll go up where the air is fresh and sweet.
I'll get away from the hustling crowd
And all that rat-race noise down in the street.

On the roof's the only place I know
Where you just have to wish to make it so.
Let's go up on the roof.

At night the stars put on a show for free,
And, darling, you can share it all with me.

I keep on tellin' you
That right smack dab in the middle of town,
I found a paradise that's trouble proof.
And if this old world starts getting' you down,
There's room enough for two up on the roof,
Way up on the roof.

Venus

Words and Music by Edward Marshall

recorded by Frankie Avalon

Hey, Venus, oh, Venus.
Hey, Venus, oh, Venus.

Venus, if you will,
Please send a little girl for me to thrill,
A girl who wants my kisses and my arms,
A girl with all the charms of you.

Venus, make her fair,
A lovely girl with sunlight in her hair,
And take the brightest stars up in the skies
And place them in her eyes for me.

Venus, goddess of love that you are,
Surely the things I ask
Can't be too great a task.

Venus, if you do,
I promise that I always will be true;
I'll give her all the love I have to give
As long as we both shall live.

Hey, Venus, oh, Venus,
Make my wish come true.
Hey, Venus, oh, Venus.
Hey, Venus, oh, Venus.

Wake Up Little Susie

Words and Music by Boudleaux Bryant and Felice Bryant

recorded by The Everly Brothers

Wake up, little Susie, wake up.
Wake up, little Susie, wake up.

We've both been sound asleep,
Wake up, little Susie and weep.
The movie's over it's four o'clock
And we're in trouble deep.

Refrain:
Wake up, little Susie, wake up little Susie,
Well, what are we gonna tell your Mama?
What are we gonna tell your Pa?
What are we gonna tell our friends when they say,
"Ooh la la"
Wake up, little Susie, wake up, little Susie.

Well, we told your Mama that we'd be in by ten.
Well, Susie baby, looks like we goofed again
Wake up, little Susie, wake up, little Susie
We've gotta go home.

The movie wasn't so hot,
It didn't have much of a plot.
We fell asleep, and our goose is cooked,
Our reputation is shot.

Refrain

Walk Like a Man

Words and Music by Bob Crewe and Bob Gaudio

recorded by The 4 Seasons

Oh, how you tried to cut me down to size,
Tellin' dirty lies to my friends.
My own father said, "Give her up, don't bother,
The world isn't coming to an end."

He said, "Walk like a man, talk like a man,
Walk like a man, my son.
No woman's worth crawlin' on the earth,
So walk like a man, my son."

Bye-aye, baby, don't mean maybe;
Gonna get along somehow.
Soon you'll be cryin', account of all your lyin',
Oh yeah, just look who's laughing now.

I'm gonna walk like a man, fast as I can,
Walk like a man from you.
I'll tell the world, forget about it, girl,
And walk like a man from you.

Walk On By

Words and Music by Kendall Hays

recorded by Leroy Van Dyke

If I see you tomorrow on some street in town,
Pardon me if I don't say "hello."
I belong to another; it wouldn't look so good
To know someone I'm not supposed to know

Refrain:
Just walk on by, wait on the corner,
I love you, but we're strangers when we meet.
Just walk on by, wait on the corner,
I love you, but we're strangers when we meet.

In a dimly lit corner in a place outside of town,
Tonight we'll try to say goodbye again.
But I know it's not over. I'll call tomorrow night.
I can't let you go, so why pretend.

Refrain

Walk Right In

Words and Music by Gus Cannon and H. Woods

recorded by The Rooftop Singers

Walk right in,
Set right down,
Daddy, let your mind roll on.
Walk right in,
Set right down,
Daddy, let your mind roll on.

Refrain:
Everybody's talkin' 'bout a new way o' walkin',
Do you wanna lose your mind?

Walk right in,
Set right down,
Daddy, let your mind roll on.

Walk right in,
Set right down,
Baby, let your hair hang down.
Walk right in,
Set right down,
Baby, let your hair hang down.

Refrain

Walk right in,
Set right down,
Baby, let your hair hang down.

The Watusi

Words and Music by Shirley Hall, Leslie Temple and James Johnson

recorded by The Vibrations

There's a dance called Watusi, it's out of sight,
First you slide to the left, then to the right.

The Watusi is out of sight,
You slide to the left, then to the right.
Take two steps up and keep it tight.
And do the Watusi, it sure is a sight.
Come on, sugar pie, keep with the beat,
And Watusi, Watusi with me.

You shimmy and shoulder and slop with your feet,
And wiggle your hips in time with the beat.
You do the Bow and Arrow, come out of the Horse,
And Pigmy Shuffle when you take your choice.
Come on, sugar pie, keep with the beat,
And Watusi, Watusi with me.

There's a dance called Watusi, it's out of sight,
First you slide to the left, then to the right.
Two steps forward, keep it tight.
There's a dance called Watusi, it's out of sight.

Don't stop now, I'm really not through.
There's so many more steps that you can do.
Well the Dish Rag, the Stiff, the Big Boy Pete,
The Double Watusi, honey, in time with the beat.
Come on try, sugar pie, it's easy to do,
And Watusi, Watusi with me.

The Way You Do the Things You Do

Words and Music by William "Smokey" Robinson and Robert Rogers

recorded by The Temptations

You got a smile so bright,
You know you could've been a candle.
I'm holding you so tight,
You know you could've been a handle.
The way you swept me off my feet,
You know you could've been a broom.
The way you smell so sweet,
You know you could've been some perfume.

Refrain:
Well, you could've been anything
That you wanted to and I can tell.
The way you do the things you do.
Ah, baby.

As pretty as you are,
You know you could've been a flower.
If good looks caused a minute,
You know that you could be an hour.
The way you stole my heart,
You know you could've been a cool crook.
And baby, you're so smart,
You know you could've been a school book.

Refrain

When I Grow Up (To Be a Man)

Words and Music by Brian Wilson and Mike Love

recorded by The Beach Boys

When I grow up to be a man,
Will I dig the same things that turn me on as a kid?
Will I look back and say that I wish I hadn't done what I did?
Will I joke around and still dig those sounds
When I grow up to be a man?

Will I look for the same things in a woman that I dig in a girl?
Will I settle down fast or will I first wanna travel the world?
Now I'm young and free, but how will it be
When I grow up to be a man?

Will my kids be proud or think their old man is really a square?
When they're out havin' fun, yeah, will I still wanna have my share?
Will I love my wife for the rest of my life
When I grow up to be a man?

What will I be
When I grow up to be a man?
Won't last forever.
Won't last forever.

Where Did Our Love Go

Words and Music by Brian Holland, Lamont Dozier and Edward Holland

recorded by The Supremes

Baby, baby, baby don't leave me.
Ooh, please don't leave me all by myself.
I've got this burning, burning, yearning feelin' inside me.
Ooh, deep inside me and it hurts so bad.

You came into my heart (baby, baby) so tenderly,
With a burning love (baby, baby)
That stings like a bee (baby, baby).
Now that I surrender (baby, baby) so helplessly,
You now want to leave (baby, baby).
Ooh, you wanna leave me (baby, baby).
Ooh (baby, baby).

Baby, baby, where did our love go?
Ooh, don't you want me?
Don't you want me no more (baby, baby)?
Ooh, baby.

Baby, baby, where did our love go?
And all your promises of a love forevermore!
I've got this burning, burning, yearning feelin' inside me.
Ooh, deep inside me, and it hurts so bad.

Before you won my heart (baby, baby)
You were a perfect guy.
But now that you got me,
You wanna leave me behind (baby, baby).
Ooh, baby.

Baby, baby, baby don't leave me.
Ooh, please don't leave me all by myself (baby, baby).
Ooh.

Where the Boys Are

Words and Music by Howard Greenfield and Neil Sedaka

recorded by Connie Francis

Where the boys are, someone waits for me;
A smiling face, a warm embrace,
Two arms to hold me tenderly.
Where the boys are, my true love will be.
He's walkin' down some street in town,
And I know he's lookin' there for me.

In the crowd of a million people,
I'll find my Valentine,
Then I'll climb to the highest steeple
And tell the world he's mine.

Till he holds me, I wait impatiently,
Where the boys are, where the boys are,
Where the boys are, someone waits for me.

Who Put the Bomp
(In the Bomp Ba Bomp Ba Bomp)

Words and Music by Barry Mann and Gerry Goffin

recorded by Barry Mann

I'd like to thank the guy who wrote the song
That made my baby fall in love with me.

Refrain:
Who put the bomp in the bomp ba bomp ba bomp?
Who put the ram in the ram-a-lam-a-ding-dong?
Who put the bop in the bop sh-bop sh-bop?
Who put the dit in the dit, dit, dit, dit-da?
Who was that man? I'd like to shake his hand.
He made my baby fall in love with me.

When my baby heard,
Bomp, ba-ba-bomp, ba-bom-ba-bomp-bomp,
Ev'ry word went right into her heart.
And when she heard them singing,
Ram-a-lam-a-lam-a-lam-a-ding-dong,
She said we'd never have to part.

Refrain

Each time that we're alone,
Bomp, ba-ba-bomp, ba-bom-ba-bomp-bomp
Sets my baby's heart all aglow.
And ev'ry time we dance to
Ram-a-lam-a-lam-a-lam-a-ding-dong,
She always says she loves me so.

Why Do Fools Fall in Love

Words and Music by Morris Levy and Frankie Lymon

recorded by Frankie Lymon & The Teenagers

Oo-wah, oo-wah,
Oo-wah, oo-wah,
Oo-wah, oo-wah.
Why do fools fall in love?

Why do birds sing so gay
And lovers await the break of day?
Why do they fall in love?
Why does the rain fall from up above?
Why do fools fall in love?
Why do they fall in love?

Love is a losing game.
Love can be a shame.
I know of a fool, you see,
For that fool is me.
Tell me why.
Tell me why.

Why do birds sing so gay
And lovers await the break of day?
Why do they fall in love?
Why does the rain fall from up above?
Why do fools fall in love?
Why do they fall in love?

Why does my heart skip a crazy beat?
For I know it will reach defeat.
Tell me why,
Tell me why,
Why do fools fall in love?

Will You Love Me Tomorrow
(Will You Still Love Me Tomorrow)

Words and Music by Gerry Goffin and Carole King

recorded by The Shirelles

Tonight you're mine completely.
You give your love so sweetly.
Tonight the light of love is in your eyes,
But will you love me tomorrow?

Is this a lasting treasure
Or just a moment's pleasure?
Can I believe the magic of your sighs?
Will you still love me tomorrow?

Tonight with words unspoken,
You say that I'm the only one.
But will my heart be broken
When the night meets the morning sun?

I'd like to know that your love
Is love that I can be sure of.
So tell me now, and I won't ask again.
Will you still love me tomorrow?
Will you still love me tomorrow?

Willie and the Hand Jive

Words and Music by Johnny Otis

recorded by Johnny Otis Show

I know a cat named Way-Out Willie.
He got a cool little chick named Rockin' Millie.
He can walk and stroll and Susie Q
And do that crazy Hand Jive, too.

Refrain:
Hand Jive, Hand Jive, Hand Jive,
Doin' that crazy Hand Jive.

Papa told Willie, "You'll ruin my home.
You and that Hand Jive has got to go.
Willie said, "Papa, don't put me down.
They're doin' the Hand Jive all over town."

Refrain

Mama, mama, look at Uncle Joe.
He's doing the Hand Jive with sister Flo.
Grandma gave baby sister a dime,
Said, "Do that Hand Jive one more time."

Refrain

Doctor and a lawyer and an Indian chief,
Now they all dig that crazy beat.
Way-Out Willie gave them all a treat
When he did that Hand Jive with his feet.

Refrain

Now Willie and Millie got married last fall.
They had a little Willie junior and that ain't all.
Well, the baby got famous in his crib, you see,
Doin, the Hand Jive on TV.

Refrain

Wooden Heart

Words and Music by Ben Weisman, Fred Wise, Kay Twomey and Berthold Kaempfert

recorded by Joe Dowell

Can't you see I love you?
Please don't break my heart in two.
That's not hard to do
'Cause I don't have a wooden heart.
And if you say good-bye
Then I know that I would cry.
Maybe I would die
'Cause I don't have a wooden heart.

There's no strings upon this love of mine.
It was always you from the start.
Treat me nice, treat me good,
Treat me like you really should,
'Cause I'm not made of wood,
And I don't have a wooden heart.

Ya Ya

Words and Music by Morris Levy and Clarence Lewis

recorded by Lee Dorsey

Oh, well, I'm sittin' here, la, la,
Waiting for my ya ya,
Uh huh, uh huh.
Er, sittin' here, la, la,
Waiting for my ya ya,
Uh huh, uh huh.
It may sound funny,
But I don't believe she's comin',
Uh huh, uh huh.

Baby, honey, don't leave me worried,
Uh huh, uh huh.
Er, baby, honey, er, don't leave me worried,
Uh huh, uh huh.
You know that I love you.
Oh, how I love you,
Uh huh, uh huh.

Yakety Yak

Words and Music by Jerry Leiber and Mike Stoller

recorded by The Coasters

Take out the papers and the trash
Or you don't get no spending cash.
If you don't scrub that kitchen floor,
You ain't gonna rock 'n' roll no more.
Yakety yak! Don't talk back.

Just finish cleaning up your room.
Let's see that dust fly with that broom.
Get all that garbage out of sight
Or you don't go out Friday night.
Yakety yak! Don't talk back.

You just put on your coat and hat
And walk yourself to the laundrymat.
And when you finish doing that,
Bring in the dog and put out the cat.
Yakety yak! Don't talk back.

Don't you give me no dirty looks.
Your father's hip; he knows what cooks.
Just tell your hoodlum friends outside,
You ain't got time to take a ride.
Yakety yak! Don't talk back.
Yakety yak, yakety yak!

You Talk Too Much

Words and Music by Reginald Hall and Joe Jones

recorded Joe Jones

You talk too much, you worry me to death,
You talk too much, you even worry my pet.
You just talk, talk too much.

You talk about people that you don't know,
You talk about people wherever you go.
You just talk, talk too much.

You talk about people that you've never seen,
You talk about people, you can make me scream.
You just talk, you talk too much.

You Win Again

Words and Music by Hank Williams

recorded by Fats Domino

The news is out, all over town,
That you've been seen a-runnin' 'round.
I know that I should leave, but then,
I just can't go, you win again.
This heart of mine could never see
What ev'rybody knew but me.
Just trusting you was my great sin.
What can I do, you win again.

I'm sorry for your victim now,
'Cause soon his head like mine will bow.
He'll give his heart but all in vain,
And someday say, you win again.
You have no heart, you have no shame,
But take true love and give the blame.
I guess that I should not complain.
I love you still, you win again.

Young Blood

Words and Music by Jerry Leiber, Mike Stoller and Doc Pomus

recorded by The Coasters

I saw her standin' on the corner,
A yellow ribbon in her hair.
I couldn't stop myself from shoutin',
"Look a-there, look a-there,
Look a-there, Look a-there!"

Refrain:
Young blood, young blood, young blood.
I can't get you out of my mind.

I took one look and I was fractured.
I tried to walk but I was lame.
I tried to talk but I just stuttered,
"What's your name, what's your name,
What's your name, What's your name?"

Refrain

What crazy stuff. She looked so tough.
I had to follow her all the way home.
Then things went bad. I met her dad.
He said, "You better leave my daughter alone."

I couldn't sleep a wink for tryin'.
I saw the risin' of the sun,
And all the night my heart was cryin',
"You're the one, you're the one,
You're the one, you're the one!"

Refrain Twice

Young Love

Words and Music by Ric Cartey

recorded by Sonny James

They say for ev'ry boy and girl
There's just one love in this old world,
And I know I found mine.
The heavenly touch of your embrace
Tells me no one can take your place
Ever in my heart.

Refrain:
Young love, first love,
Filled with true devotion.
Young love, our love
We share with deep emotion.

Just one kiss from your sweet lips
Will tell me that your love is real,
And I can feel that it's true.
We will vow to one another
There will never be another
Love for you or for me.

Refrain

Artist Index

The Angels
110 My Boyfriend's Back

Eddy Arnold
106 Make the World Go Away

Frankie Avalon
26 A Boy Without a Girl
189 Venus

The Beach Boys
13 Barbara Ann
15 Be True to Your School
47 Don't Worry Baby
53 Fun, Fun, Fun
76 I Get Around
96 Little Deuce Coupe
166 Surfin' U.S.A.
196 When I Grow Up (To Be a Man)

The Beatles
33 Chains
91 Kansas City
124 Please Mr. Postman
186 Twist and Shout

Chuck Berry
113 No Particular Place to Go

Big Bopper
35 Chantilly Lace

Marcie Blane
24 Bobby's Girl

Pat Boone
34 Chains of Love
74 I Almost Lost My Mind
183 Tutti Frutti

Jimmy Bowen
83 I'm Stickin' with You

The Brothers Four
61 Greenfields

The Cadillacs
158 Speedoo

Freddy Cannon
121 Palisades Park

Johnny Cash
81 I Walk the Line

Richard Chamberlain
9 All I Have to Do Is Dream

Ray Charles
75 I Can't Stop Loving You

Chubby Checker
94 Limbo Rock
185 The Twist

The Cheers
21 Black Denim Trousers and
　　Motorcycle Boots

The Chiffons
119 One Fine Day

The Chordettes
99 Lollipop

The Chords
141 Sh-Boom (Life Could Be a
　　Dream)

Dee Clark
125 Raindrops

The Clovers
103 Love Potion Number 9

The Coasters
36 Charlie Brown
205 Yakety Yak
208 Young Blood

The Cookies
33 Chains

The Crests
155 Sixteen Candles

The Crew-Cuts
50 Earth Angel
141 Sh-Boom (Life Could Be a
　　Dream)

The Crickets
88 It's So Easy
107 Maybe Baby
114 Oh Boy!
175 That'll Be the Day

The Crystals
65 He's a Rebel

Danny & The Juniors
11 At the Hop
128 Rock and Roll Is Here to Stay

Bobby Darin
49 Dream Lover
159 Splish Splash
178 Things

Jimmy Dean
18 Big Bad John

The Diamonds
150 Silhouettes

Bo Diddley
23 Bo Diddley

Mark Dinning
172 Teen Angel

Dion
133 Ruby Baby

Dion & The Belmonts
173 A Teenager in Love

Carl Dobkins, Jr.
112 My Heart Is an Open Book

Fats Domino
207 You Win Again

Lee Dorsey
204 Ya Ya

Joe Dowell
203 Wooden Heart

The Drifters
118 On Broadway
137 Save the Last Dance for Me
177 There Goes My Baby
187 Under the Boardwalk
188 Up on the Roof

Paul Evans
154 (Seven Little Girls) Sitting in the
　　Back Seat

Betty Everett
144 The Shoop Shoop Song
　　(It's in His Kiss)

The Everly Brothers
9 All I Have to Do Is Dream
29 Bye Bye Love
32 Cathy's Clown
38 Crying in the Rain
42 Devoted to You
79 ('Til) I Kissed You
190 Wake Up Little Susie

The Exciters
174 Tell Her (Tell Him)

Fabian
182 Turn Me Loose

The Five Satins
84 In the Still of the Nite
　　(I'll Remember)

The Four Lads
108 Moments to Remember

The Four Preps
184 26 Miles (Santa Catalina)

The 4 Seasons
20 Big Girls Don't Cry
143 Sherry
191 Walk Like a Man

Connie Francis
51 Ev'rybody's Somebody's Fool
95 Lipstick on Your Collar
163 Stupid Cupid
198 Where the Boys Are

Don Gibson
116 Oh, Lonesome Me

Lesley Gore
85 It's My Party

Bill Haley & His Comets
129 Rock Around the Clock
142 Shake, Rattle and Roll

George Hamilton IV
131 A Rose and a Baby Ruth

Wilbert Harrison
91 Kansas City

Herman's Hermits
150 Silhouettes

Buddy Holly
52 Everyday
123 Peggy Sue

Brian Hyland
140 Sealed with a Kiss

The Isley Brothers
148 Shout
186 Twist and Shout

Sonny James
209 Young Love

Jan & Dean
40 Dead Man's Curve
97 The Little Old Lady
(From Pasadena)
147 Sidewalk Surfin'
165 Surf City

Joe Jones
206 You Talk Too Much

Ben E. King
160 Stand by Me

The Kingston Trio
138 Scotch and Soda

Buddy Knox with The Rhythm Orchids
122 Party Doll

Steve Lawrence
55 Go Away, Little Girl

Jerry Lee Lewis
58 Great Balls of Fire

Little Anthony & The Imperials
170 Tears on My Pillow

Little Eva
98 The Loco-Motion

Little Richard
105 Lucille
126 Ready Teddy
183 Tutti Frutti

Jim Lowe
60 The Green Door

Frankie Lymon & The Teenagers
8 The ABC's of Love
200 Why Do Fools Fall in Love

Barry Mann
199 Who Put the Bomp (In the Bomp Ba Bomp Ba Bomp)

Manfred Mann
44 Do Wah Diddy Diddy

Martha & The Vandellas
39 Dancing in the Street
67 Heatwave (Love Is Like a Heatwave)

The Marvelettes
16 Beechwood 4-5789
124 Please Mr. Postman

Jimmy McGriff
77 I Got a Woman

The McGuire Sisters
57 Goodnight My Love, Pleasant Dreams
152 Sincerely
164 Sugartime

The Miracles
145 Shop Around

Guy Mitchell
153 Singing the Blues

The Monotones
25 Book of Love

The Mystics
73 Hushabye

Ricky Nelson
68 Hello Mary Lou
181 Travelin' Man

The Newbeats
27 Bread and Butter

Roy Orbison
37 Crying
48 Dream Baby (How Long Must I Dream)
117 Oh, Pretty Woman
120 Only the Lonely (Know the Way I Feel)

Johnny Otis Show
202 Willie and the Hand Jive

The Paris Sisters
80 I Love How You Love Me

Paul & Paula
69 Hey Paula

The Penguins
50 Earth Angel

Carl Perkins
22 Blue Suede Shoes

Phil Phillips with The Twilights
139 Sea of Love

The Platters
59 The Great Pretender

The Playmates
17 Beep Beep

Elvis Presley
10 All Shook Up
22 Blue Suede Shoes
31 Can't Help Falling in Love
45 Don't
46 Don't Be Cruel (To a Heart That's True)
56 Good Luck Charm
66 Heartbreak Hotel
72 Hound Dog
78 I Got Stung
82 I Want You, I Need You, I Love You
86 It's Now or Never
89 Jailhouse Rock
101 Love Me
102 Love Me Tender
104 Loving You
126 Ready Teddy
127 Return to Sender
162 Stuck on You
167 Surrender
171 (Let Me Be Your) Teddy Bear
180 Too Much

The Rays
150 Silhouettes

Jim Reeves
64 He'll Have to Go

Songwriter Index

Kal Mann
171 (Let Me Be Your) Teddy Bear

John Marascalco
57 Goodnight My Love, Pleasant
Dreams
126 Ready Teddy

Edward Marshall
189 Venus

Lennie Martin
151 Since I Don't Have You
179 This I Swear

Vera Matson
102 Love Me Tender

Ellas McDaniel
23 Bo Diddley

J. Leslie McFarland
162 Stuck on You

Floyd McRae
141 Sh-Boom (Life Could Be a
Dream)

Phil Medley
186 Twist and Shout

Joe Melson
37 Crying
120 Only the Lonely (Know the Way
I Feel)

Bob Merrill
71 Honeycomb

Frank Miller
61 Greenfields

Fleecie Moore
93 Let the Good Times Roll

Marvin Moore
60 The Green Door

George Motola
57 Goodnight My Love, Pleasant
Dreams

Maurice Mysels
82 I Want You, I Need You,
I Love You

Jack Nance
87 It's Only Make Believe

Esther Navarro
158 Speedoo

Ben E. Nelson
177 There Goes My Baby

A. Nugetre
34 Chains of Love

Roy Orbison
37 Crying
117 Oh, Pretty Woman
120 Only the Lonely (Know the Way
I Feel)

Ann Orlowski
132 Rubber Ball

Johnny Otis
202 Willie and the Hand Jive

Larry Parks
27 Bread and Butter

Fred Parris
84 In the Still of the Nite
(I'll Remember)

Charles Patrick
25 Book of Love

Lover Patterson
177 There Goes My Baby

Little Richard Penniman
105 Lucille
183 Tutti Frutti

Hugo Peretti
31 Can't Help Falling in Love

Carl Lee Perkins
22 Blue Suede Shoes

Norman Petty
52 Everyday
88 It's So Easy
107 Maybe Baby
114 Oh Boy!
123 Peggy Sue
175 That'll Be the Day

Charles Phillips
164 Sugartime

Gene Pitney
65 He's a Rebel
68 Hello Mary Lou

Lee Pockriss
112 My Heart Is an Open Book
154 (Seven Little Girls) Sitting in the
Back Seat

Doc Pomus
73 Hushabye
137 Save the Last Dance for Me
167 Surrender
168 Suspicion
173 A Teenager in Love
182 Turn Me Loose
208 Young Blood

Bill Post
156 Sixteen Reasons (Why I Love
You)

Doree Post
156 Sixteen Reasons (Why I Love
You)

Elvis Presley
10 All Shook Up
46 Don't Be Cruel (To a Heart
That's True)
66 Heartbreak Hotel
102 Love Me Tender

Buck Ram
59 The Great Pretender

Artie Resnick
187 Under the Boardwalk

J.P. Richardson
35 Chantilly Lace

Johnny Roberts
109 My Boy Lollipop

William "Smokey" Robinson
111 My Guy
145 Shop Around
195 The Way You Do the Things
You Do

Joseph Rock
151 Since I Don't Have You
179 This I Swear

Robert Rogers
195 The Way You Do the Things
You Do

Lee Rosenberg
180 Too Much

Beverly Ross
99 Lollipop

Bert Russell
174 Tell Her (Tell Him)
186 Twist and Shout

More Collections from The Lyric Library

BROADWAY VOLUME I

An invaluable collection of lyrics to 200 top Broadway tunes, including: All at Once You Love Her • All I Ask of You • And All That Jazz • Any Dream Will Do • As Long As He Needs Me • At the End of the Day • Autumn in New York • Bali Ha'i • Bewitched • Cabaret • Castle on a Cloud • Climb Ev'ry Mountain • Comedy Tonight • Don't Rain on My Parade • Everything's Coming up Roses • Hello, Dolly! • I Could Have Danced All Night • I Dreamed a Dream • I Remember It Well • If I Were a Bell • It's the Hard-Knock Life • Let Me Entertain You • Mame • My Funny Valentine • Oklahoma • Seasons of Love • September Song • Seventy Six Trombones • Shall We Dance? • Springtime for Hitler • Summer Nights • Tomorrow • Try to Remember • Unexpected Song • What I Did for Love • With One Look • You'll Never Walk Alone • (I Wonder Why?) You're Just in Love • and more.

_____00240201 ....$14.95

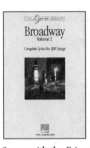

BROADWAY VOLUME II

200 more favorite Broadway lyrics (with no duplication from Volume I): Ain't Misbehavin' • All of You • Another Op'nin', Another Show • As If We Never Said Goodbye • Beauty School Dropout • The Best of Times • Bring Him Home • Brotherhood of Man • Camelot • Close Every Door • Consider Yourself • Do-Re-Mi • Edelweiss • Getting to Know You • Have You Met Miss Jones? • I Loved You Once in Silence • I'm Flying • If Ever I Would Leave You • The Impossible Dream (The Quest) • It Only Takes a Moment • The Lady Is a Tramp • The Last Night of the World • A Little More Mascara • Lost in the Stars • Love Changes Everything • Me and My Girl • Memory • My Heart Belongs to Daddy • On a Clear Day (You Can See Forever) • On My Own • People • Satin Doll • The Sound of Music • Sun and Moon • The Surrey with the Fringe on Top • Unusual Way (In a Very Unusual Way) • We Kiss in a Shadow • We Need a Little Christmas • Who Will Buy? • Wishing You Were Somehow Here Again • Younger Than Springtime • and more.

_____00240205 ....$14.95

CHRISTMAS

200 lyrics to the most loved Christmas songs of all time, including: Angels We Have Heard on High • Auld Lang Syne • Away in a Manger • Baby, It's Cold Outside • The Chipmunk Song • The Christmas Shoes • The Christmas Song (Chestnuts Roasting on an Open Fire) • Christmas Time Is Here • Do They Know It's Christmas? • Do You Hear What I Hear • Feliz Navidad • The First Noel • Frosty the Snow Man • The Gift • God Rest Ye Merry, Gentlemen • Goin' on a Sleighride • Grandma Got Run over by a Reindeer • Happy Xmas (War Is Over) • He Is Born, the Holy Child (Il Est Ne, Le Divin Enfant) • The Holly and the Ivy • A Holly Jolly Christmas • (There's No Place Like) Home for the Holidays • I Heard the Bells on Christmas Day • I Wonder As I Wander • I'll Be Home for Christmas • I've Got My Love to Keep Me Warm • In the Bleak Midwinter • It Came upon the Midnight Clear • It's Beginning to Look like Christmas • It's Just Another New Year's Eve • Jingle Bells • Joy to the World • Mary, Did You Know? • Merry Christmas, Darling • The Most Wonderful Time of the Year • My Favorite Things • Rudolph the Red-Nosed Reindeer • Silent Night • Silver Bells • The Twelve Days of Christmas • What Child Is This? • What Made the Baby Cry? • Wonderful Christmastime • and more.

_____00240206 ....$14.95

See our website for a complete contents list for each volume:
www.halleonard.com

FOR MORE INFORMATION, SEE YOUR LOCAL MUSIC DEALER,
OR WRITE TO:

7777 W. BLUEMOUND RD. P.O. BOX 13819 MILWAUKEE, WI 53213

Prices, contents and availability subject to change without notice.

More Collections from The Lyric Library

CLASSIC ROCK

Lyrics to 200 essential rock classics songs, including: All Day and All of the Night • All Right Now • Angie • Another One Bites the Dust • Back in the U.S.S.R. • Ballroom Blitz • Barracuda • Beast of Burden • Bell Bottom Blues • Brain Damage • Brass in Pocket • Breakdown • Breathe • Bus Stop • California Girls • Carry on Wayward Son • Centerfold • Changes • Cocaine • Cold As Ice • Come Sail Away • Come Together • Crazy Little Thing Called Love • Crazy on You • Don't Do Me like That • Don't Fear the Reaper • Don't Let the Sun Go down on Me • Don't Stand So Close to Me • Dreamer • Drive My Car • Dust in the Wind • 867-5309/Jenny • Emotional Rescue • Every Breath You Take • Every Little Thing She Does Is Magic • Eye in the Sky • Eye of the Tiger • Fame • Forever Young • Fortress Around Your Heart • Free Ride • Give a Little Bit • Gloria • Godzilla • Green-Eyed Lady • Heartache Tonight • Heroes • Hey Joe • Hot Blooded • I Fought the Law • I Shot the Sheriff • I Won't Back Down • Instant Karma • Invisible Touch • It's Only Rock 'N' Roll (But I like It) • It's Still Rock and Roll to Me • Layla • The Logical Song • Long Cool Woman (In a Black Dress) • Love Hurts • Maggie May • Me and Bobby McGee • Message in a Bottle • Mississippi Queen • Money • Money for Nothing • My Generation • New Kid in Town • Nights in White Satin • Paradise by the Dashboard Light • Piano Man • Rebel, Rebel • Refugee • Rhiannon • Roxanne • Shattered • Smoke on the Water • Sultans of Swing • Sweet Emotion • Walk This Way • We Gotta Get Out of This Place • We Will Rock You • Wouldn't It Be Nice • and many more!

_____00240183 ....$14.95

CONTEMPORARY CHRISTIAN

An amazing collection of 200 lyrics from some of the most prominent Contemporary Christian artists: Abba (Father) • After the Rain • Angels • Awesome God • Breathe on Me • Circle of Friends • Doubly Good to You • Down on My Knees • El Shaddai • Father's Eyes • Friends • Give It Away • Go Light Your World • God's Own Fool • Grand Canyon • The Great Adventure • The Great Divide • He Walked a Mile • Heaven and Earth • Heaven in the Real World • His Strength Is Perfect • Household of Faith • How Beautiful • I Surrender All • Jesus Freak • Joy in the Journey • Judas' Kiss • A Little More • Live Out Loud • Love Will Be Our Home • A Maze of Grace • The Message • My Utmost for His Highest • Oh Lord, You're Beautiful • People Need the Lord • Pray • Say the Name • Signs of Life • Speechless • Stand • Steady On • Via Dolorosa • The Warrior Is a Child • What Matters Most • Would I Know You • and more.

_____00240184 ....$14.95

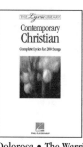

COUNTRY

A great resource of lyrics to 200 of the best country songs of all time, including: Act Naturally • All My Ex's Live in Texas • All the Gold in California • Always on My Mind • Amazed • American Made • Angel of the Morning • Big Bad John • Blue • Blue Eyes Crying in the Rain • Boot Scootin' Boogie • Breathe • By the Time I Get to Phoenix • Could I Have This Dance • Crazy • Daddy's Hands • D-I-V-O-R-C-E • Down at the Twist and Shout • Elvira • Folsom Prison Blues • Friends in Low Places • The Gambler • Grandpa (Tell Me 'Bout the Good Old Days) • Harper Valley P.T.A. • He Thinks He'll Keep Her • Hey, Good Lookin' • I Fall to Pieces • I Hope You Dance • I Love a Rainy Night • I Saw the Light • I've Got a Tiger by the Tail • Islands in the Stream • Jambalaya (On the Bayou) • The Keeper of the Stars • King of the Road • Lucille • Make the World Go Away • Mammas Don't Let Your Babies Grow up to Be Cowboys • My Baby Thinks He's a Train • Okie from Muskogee • Ring of Fire • Rocky Top • Sixteen Tons • Stand by Me • There's a Tear in My Beer • Walkin' After Midnight • When You Say Nothing at All • Where the Stars and Stripes and the Eagle Fly • Where Were You (When the World Stopped Turning) • You Are My Sunshine • Your Cheatin' Heart • and more.

_____00240204 ....$14.95

See our website for a complete contents list for each volume:
www.halleonard.com

FOR MORE INFORMATION, SEE YOUR LOCAL MUSIC DEALER,
OR WRITE TO:

HAL•LEONARD®
CORPORATION

7777 W. BLUEMOUND RD. P.O. BOX 13819 MILWAUKEE, WI 53213

More Collections from The Lyric Library

EARLY ROCK 'N' ROLL

Lyrics to 200 top songs that started the rock 'n' roll revolution, including: All I Have to Do Is Dream • All Shook Up • At the Hop • Baby Love • Barbara Ann • Be-Bop-A-Lula • Big Girls Don't Cry • Blue Suede Shoes • Bo Diddley • Book of Love • Calendar Girl • Chantilly Lace • Charlie Brown • Crying • Dancing in the Street • Do Wah Diddy Diddy • Don't Be Cruel (To a Heart That's True) • Earth Angel • Fun, Fun, Fun • Great Balls of Fire • He's a Rebel • Heatwave (Love Is like a Heatwave) • Hello Mary Lou • Hound Dog • I Walk the Line • It's My Party • Kansas City • The Loco-Motion • My Boyfriend's Back • My Guy • Oh, Pretty Woman • Peggy Sue • Rock and Roll Is Here to Stay • Sixteen Candles • Splish Splash • Stand by Me • Stupid Cupid • Surfin' U.S.A. • Teen Angel • A Teenager in Love • Twist and Shout • Walk like a Man • Where the Boys Are • Why Do Fools Fall in Love • Willie and the Hand Jive • and more.

_____00240203 ....$14.95

LOVE SONGS

Lyrics to 200 of the most romantic songs ever written, including: All My Loving • Always in My Heart (Siempre En Mi Corazon) • And I Love Her • Anniversary Song • Beautiful in My Eyes • Call Me Irresponsible • Can You Feel the Love Tonight • Cheek to Cheek • (They Long to Be) Close to You • Could I Have This Dance • Dedicated to the One I Love • Don't Know Much • Dream a Little Dream of Me • Endless Love • Fields of Gold • For Once in My Life • Grow Old with Me • The Hawaiian Wedding Song (Ke Kali Nei Au) • Heart and Soul • Hello, Young Lovers • How Deep Is the Ocean (How High Is the Sky) • I Just Called to Say I Love You • I'll Be There • I've Got My Love to Keep Me Warm • Just the Way You Are • Longer • L-O-V-E • Love Will Keep Us Together • Misty • Moonlight in Vermont • More (Ti Guardero' Nel Cuore) • My Funny Valentine • My Heart Will Go on (Love Theme from 'Titanic') • She • Speak Softly, Love (Love Theme) • Till • A Time for Us (Love Theme) • Unchained Melody • Up Where We Belong • We've Only Just Begun • What the World Needs Now Is Love • When I Fall in Love • Witchcraft • Wonderful Tonight • You Are the Sunshine of My Life • You're the Inspiration • You've Made Me So Very Happy • and more!

_____00240186 ....$14.95

POP/ROCK BALLADS

Lyrics to 200 top tunes of the pop/rock era, including: Adia • After the Love Has Gone • Against All Odds (Take a Look at Me Now) • Always on My Mind • Amazed • And So It Goes • Baby What a Big Surprise • Ben • Breathe • Change the World • Come to My Window • Do You Know Where You're Going To? • Don't Cry Out Loud • Don't Fall in Love with a Dreamer • Easy • Feelings (?Dime?) • Fire and Rain • From a Distance • Georgia on My Mind • Hero • I Hope You Dance • Imagine • In the Air Tonight • Iris • Just My Imagination (Running Away with Me) • Killing Me Softly with His Song • Laughter in the Rain • Looks like We Made It • My Heart Will Go on (Love Theme from 'Titanic') • New York State of Mind • The Rainbow Connection • Rainy Days and Mondays • Sailing • She's Always a Woman • Sing • Sunshine on My Shoulders • Take Me Home, Country Roads • Tears in Heaven • There You'll Be • Time After Time • Vision of Love • The Way We Were • Woman in Love • You're the Inspiration • You've Got a Friend • and more.

_____00240187 ....$14.95

See our website for a complete contents list for each volume:
www.halleonard.com

FOR MORE INFORMATION, SEE YOUR LOCAL MUSIC DEALER,
OR WRITE TO:

HAL•LEONARD®
CORPORATION

7777 W. BLUEMOUND RD. P.O. BOX 13819 MILWAUKEE, WI 53213

Prices, contents and availability subject to change without notice.